CORE SKILLS

W9-AHH-785

Math

ISBN 0-7398-5726-6

2002 Edition, Steck-Vaughn Company
Copyright © by Harcourt, Inc.

5 6 7 8 9 054 06 05

STECK-VAUGHN
ELEMENTARY · SECONDARY · ADULT · LIBRARY
A Harcourt Company

www.svschoolsupply.com

Core Skills: Math
Grade 4
Table of Contents

Core Skills: Math, Grade 4, Table of Contents (cont.)

Core Skills: Math, Grade 4, Table of Contents (cont.)

Exploring Numbers to Thousands

Complete to name each number.

1.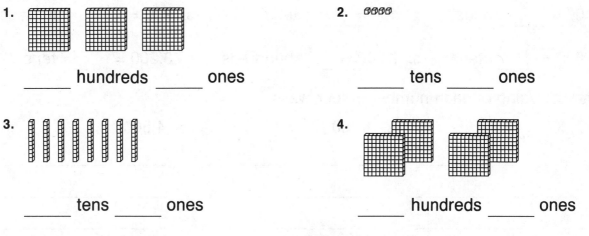

_____ hundreds _____ ones

2. _____ tens _____ ones

3. _____ tens _____ ones

4. _____ hundreds _____ ones

Here are some statements about 1,000. Write *true* or *false.* Think about what seems reasonable.

5. There are more than 1,000 pages in your math book.

_____

6. There are fewer than 1,000 fish in the Atlantic Ocean.

_____

7. There are fewer than 1,000 grains in a tablespoon of rice.

_____

8. There are more than 1,000 inches in a mile.

_____

9. There are more than 1,000 hairs on a gerbil.

_____

10. There are fewer than 1,000 letters on the front page of a newspaper.

_____

EVERYDAY MATH CONNECTION

Write the number of pennies that would equal each amount of money.

11.

_____ pennies

12.

_____ pennies

13.

_____ pennies

Mental Math
Names for Numbers

Complete.

1. 60 = _____ ones
2. 400 = _____ tens
3. 900 = _____ hundreds
4. 800 = _____ tens
5. 7,000 = _____ hundreds
6. 3,200 = _____ tens

Write the value of each number in four ways.

7. 3,800

8. 1,400

9. 4,500

_____   _____   _____

_____   _____   _____

_____   _____   _____

_____   _____   _____

Mixed Applications

10. Mr. Elliot added 6,300 gallons of water to the pool at Wayne Park. Write four different names for this number.

_____

_____

_____

_____

11. Adding 3,700 gallons of water to the pool at Regent Park made the water deep enough for diving. Write four different names for this number.

_____

_____

_____

_____

NUMBER SENSE

Complete the number patterns.

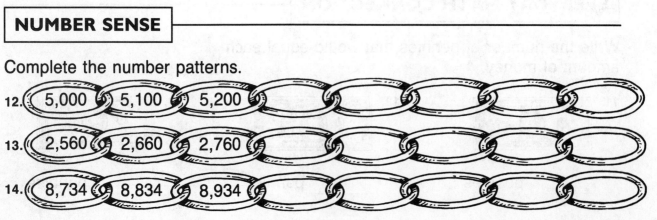

12. 5,000 5,100 5,200

13. 2,560 2,660 2,760

14. 8,734 8,834 8,934

2

Number Sense
Expressing Numbers

Express each number in two other ways.

1. 10,000 + 600 + 7

   _____

   _____

2. ninety thousand, five hundred

   _____

   _____

3. 34,069

   _____

   _____

4. 7,000 + 800 + 60 + 4

   _____

   _____

5. four thousand, six hundred seventy-three

   _____

   _____

6. 20,483

   _____

   _____

Mixed Applications

7. The longest river in the United States is the Mississippi River. It is 2,348 miles long. Write the number in words.

   _____

   _____

8. The longest river in China is the Yangtze River. It is three thousand, nine hundred fifteen miles long. Write the number in standard form.

   _____

NUMBER SENSE

Think of place-value blocks. Write the number and kind of blocks you could use for each of the following.

9. Show 7,020 using only tens.

   _____

10. Show 11,100 using only hundreds.

    _____

11. Show 231 using the same number of tens and ones.

    _____

12. Show 12,132 using the same number of thousands, tens, and ones.

    _____

Problem Solving

Use a Table

Beth recorded the number of books read by the members of the library club during October. Use the table she made to answer the questions.

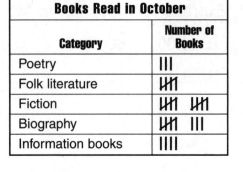

Books Read in October	
Category	Number of Books
Poetry	III
Folk literature	IIII I
Fiction	IIII I IIII I
Biography	IIII I III
Information books	IIII

1. In which category were the most books read?

   _____

2. In which category were the fewest books read?

   _____

3. How many biographies did members of the library club read in October?

   _____

Mixed Applications

Evan made a tally table. It shows the number of fiction books read by the library club during one month. Use the table to answer Exercises 4–6.

Fiction Books Read	
Type	Number
Fantasies	II
Adventure stories	IIII I II
Animal stories	III
Life in other countries	IIII I III
Historical fiction	IIII
Mystery and detective	IIII I IIII I
Science fiction	IIII I IIII I

4. How many historical fiction books were read?

   _____

5. How many adventure stories were read?

   _____

6. In which types of fiction were the same number of books read?

   _____

WRITER'S CORNER

7. Suppose you want to know what kind of books your friends have read in the last month. Describe how you would gather and display the information.

   _____

   _____

Place Value
to Hundred Thousands

Write the value of the digit 4 in each number.

1. 3,456

2. 48,062

3. 59,241

4. 497,216

_____   _____   _____   _____

_____   _____

Write the value of the underlined digit.

5. 4<u>3</u>7,215

6. 96,3<u>0</u>7

7. 4<u>8</u>,162

8. <u>9</u>76,002

_____   _____   _____   _____

_____   _____   _____

9. Express the number eight hundred fourteen
   thousand, two hundred six in two other ways.

_____

Mixed Applications

10. How many zeros must you write
    beside the digit 4 to show a
    value of forty thousand? Write
    the number.

    _____

11. Two hundred eighty-nine thousand,
    three hundred people live in
    Newton. Write the number in
    standard form and in expanded
    form.

    _____

    _____

LOGICAL REASONING

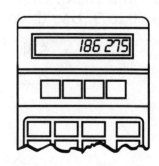

12. Enter the number 186,275 into a calculator.
    You can change the 6 to a 0 by using one
    operation—subtracting 6,000. All the other digits
    remain the same. Write how you can make these
    changes in one operation.

    a. the 8 to a 4 _____   b. the 7 to a 9 _____

Place Value to Millions

Name the period shown by the underlined digits.

1. 1,<u>667</u>,495

2. <u>657</u>,604,980

3. 258,418,<u>732</u>

_____   _____   _____

Write the number that is 1,000,000 more.

4. 67,016,018 _____

5. 639,540,086 _____

Write the number that is 10,000,000 less.

6. 23,579,410 _____

7. 845,270,100 _____

Mixed Applications

Study the number in the box. Write *true* or *false*.

18 million, 6 hundred

8. The standard form is 18,600.

_____

9. The expanded form is 10,000,000 + 8,000,000 + 600.

_____

10. The digit in the thousands place is 6.

_____

11. The value of the digit in the hundred-thousands place is 0.

_____

LOGICAL REASONING

12. In a secret code, a letter stands for each digit from 0 to 9. Use the clues to complete the code.

   Clues: a. ABH < DBH   b. DJ > DC

   D = _____   C = _____

Code	
A = 7	B = 3
C = ?	D = ?
E = 5	F = 4
G = 0	H = 9
I = 6	J = 2

Comparing Whole Numbers

Compare. Write <, or >, or = for ◯.

1. 2,541 ◯ 986
2. 274 ◯ 279
3. 8,642 ◯ 764

4. 2,329 ◯ 3,329
5. 62,911 ◯ 58,012
6. 8,116 ◯ 18,611

Write the numbers using the symbol that means *is less than.*

7. 52; 56
8. 76; 67
9. 1,339; 1,239

_____
_____
_____

Write the numbers using the symbol that means *is greater than.*

10. 84; 48
11. 2,049; 2,094
12. 26,784; 26,847

_____
_____
_____

Mixed Applications

13. Sharon hiked 1,875 meters to a lookout on Mount Royal. The peak is 1,000 meters higher than the lookout. Write the height of the peak.

_____

14. Gina's hiking club climbed 1,024 meters today. On the day before, they climbed 100 meters less than this. Write the number of meters they climbed yesterday.

_____

GEOGRAPHY CONNECTION

Use the table to answer the questions.

15. Which mountain is the highest?

_____

16. Which mountain is the lowest?

_____

17. Which mountain is higher, Mount Shasta or Mount Rainier?

_____

Heights of Some U.S. Mountains	
Mountain	**Height in Meters**
Mount Shasta	4,317
Mount Rushmore	1,745
Mount McKinley	6,194
Mount Hood	3,426
Mount Rainier	4,392
Mount Whitney	4,418

Ordering Whole Numbers

Complete the number line for each set of numbers.
Then write each group of numbers in order from least
to greatest.

1. 495; 487; 493

   ___ < ___ < ___

   485 _____ 495

2. 850, 500, 350, 650

   ___ < ___ < ___ < ___

   100 _____ 1,000

3. 880, 840, 820, 890

   ___ < ___ < ___ < ___

   800 _____ 900

Write each group of numbers in order from
least to greatest.

4. 785; 763; 812

5. 175; 136; 149

6. 4,618; 4,390; 4,364

7. 959; 990; 995; 929

8. 7,642; 7,640; 7,697; 7,604

Mixed Applications

9. The size of Acadia National Park
   in Maine is 41,409 acres. The
   size of Mesa Verde National
   Park in Colorado is 52,085 acres.
   Which park is larger?

10. The size of Zion National Park in
    Utah is 146,598 acres. Use the
    information in Exercise 9 to write
    the three national parks in order
    from greatest to least according
    to their sizes.

| LOGICAL REASONING |

Write a digit in the ☐ to make each number sentence true.

11. 2,5 ☐ 4 > 2,584

12. 8, ☐ 27 < 8,124

13. 48, ☐ 56 < 48,147

8

Problem-Solving Strategy
Find a Pattern

When you look at a pattern, think about the order, size, and position of the figures.

Draw the next four figures for each pattern.

1. _____

2. _____

3. _____

4. _____

Eric has a puzzle for his classmates. When he says 25, the answer is 125. When he says 56, the answer is 156. When he says 82, the answer is 182.

5. What is the pattern?

   _____

6. If the answer is 198, what does Eric say?

   _____

7. Pat is 48 inches tall, Clara is 39 inches tall, and June is 2 inches taller than Clara. Put the girls in order from shortest to tallest.

   _____

8. Carlos practices on his guitar for 1 hour every school day and for 2 hours each weekend day. Write the pattern he follows.

   _____

MIXED REVIEW

Write in expanded form.

1. 856 _____
2. 4,315 _____
3. 90,507 _____

Write the number that is 10,000 more.

4. 56,702 _____
5. 174,913 _____
6. 2,397,854 _____

9

Ordinal Numbers

Write the next ordinal number in words.

1. twenty-second

_____

2. eighty-seventh

_____

3. thirtieth

_____

4. fifty-sixth

_____

5. ninety-fifth

_____

6. sixty-fourth

_____

Write the missing ordinal numbers.

7. 36th, _____, 38th, 39th, _____

8. 10th, 20th, _____, _____, _____, 60th

9. 88th, _____, _____, 91st, 92nd

10. 71st, 73rd, _____, 77th, _____, 81st

Write the missing number or numbers.

11. 2, 4, 6, _____, 10, 12

12. 3, 6, _____, 12, _____, _____, 21

13. second, fifth, _____, eleventh

Use the calendar to answer Exercises 14–15. What is the day of the week of

14. November 14th? _____

15. November 22nd? _____

NOVEMBER						
S	M	T	W	Th	F	S
				1	2	3
4	5	6	7	8	9	10
11	12	13	14	15	16	17
18	19	20	21	22	23	24
25	26	27	28	29	30	

Mixed Applications

16. Mark is going to a party on the first Sunday in November. What is the date of the party? Use the calendar above.

_____

17. Tai is fifth in line. Yoko is right in front of him. What is Yoko's place in line?

_____

LOGICAL REASONING

18. Juan is directly in front of the ninth person in line. How many people are in front of Juan?

_____

19. Kate is first in line. Jeff is last in line. Emily is between Fred and Julio. Fred is behind Kate. In what place is Emily?

_____

Estimate by Rounding Numbers

Estimate by rounding to the nearest ten or to the nearest ten cents.

1. 52 _____
2. $3.78 _____
3. 66 _____
4. $1.45 _____

5. 87 _____
6. $1.34 _____
7. 555 _____
8. 226 _____

Estimate by rounding to the nearest hundred or to the nearest dollar.

9. 457 _____
10. 242 _____
11. $8.46 _____
12. 233 _____

Estimate by rounding to the nearest thousand.

13. 6,816 _____
14. 2,310 _____
15. 2,737 _____
16. 1,421 _____

Mixed Applications

17. The world's longest river is the Nile. It is about 4,160 miles long. Estimate the length to the nearest hundred miles.

_____

18. The length of the Potomac River when rounded to the nearest ten miles is 380 miles. What is the least length and the greatest length in miles that it could be?

_____

SOCIAL STUDIES CONNECTION

Each statement contains a measurement that has been rounded to the nearest ten miles. Find the exact length in the box, and write it next to the correct statement. You will not use all the numbers in the box.

Actual Lengths of Rivers in Miles
428
496
1,459
1,488
2,201
2,194

19. More than 30 bridges cross the 500-mile-long Seine River in France.

_____

20. The longest river in Europe is the Volga. It is about 2,190 miles long.

_____

21. The Arkansas River created many canyons in the United States. It is about 1,460 miles long.

_____

Mental Math
Addition Fact Strategies

Find the sum. Name the addition-fact strategy.

Counting On	Zero	Doubles	Doubles Plus One

1. 7 + 0 = ☐

_____

2. 9 + 9 = ☐

_____

3. 7 + 8 = ☐

_____

4. 6 + 1 = ☐

_____

5. 3 + 3 = ☐

_____

6. 4 + 3 = ☐

_____

7. 0 + 9 = ☐

_____

8. 5 + 6 = ☐

_____

Find the sum.

9.   0
  +5

10.   9
  +1

11.   9
  +8

12.   8
  +3

13.   1
  +5

14.   2
  +9

15.   6
  +7

16.   8
  +8

17. 9 + 2 = ___

18. 0 + 6 = ___

19. 4 + 3 = ___

20. 3 + 3 = ___

Mixed Applications

21. Marcy bought 3 birthday cards and 6 thank-you cards. How many cards did she buy?

_____

22. Campbell's Card Shop ran a sale for 6 hours on Saturday and for 5 hours on Sunday. For how many hours did the sale run?

_____

LOGICAL REASONING

23. Follow the rule. Complete.

Add 5	
Input	Output
1	6
3	
5	
6	

Add 8	
Input	Output
9	
8	
7	
3	

24. Write the rule. Complete.

Input	Output
4	6
5	7
6	
7	

Input	Output
0	9
2	11
	17
	18

Mental Math
Grouping Addends

Find the sum. Check by grouping the addends differently.

1. $3 + (5 + 4) = \boxed{}$

2. $(2 + 7) + 8 = \boxed{}$

3. $4 + (1 + 8) = \boxed{}$

4. $(4 + 5) + 6 = \boxed{}$

5. $9 + (2 + 7) = \boxed{}$

6. $(7 + 3) + 4 = \boxed{}$

Look for tens. Find the sum.

7.	8.	9.	10.	11.	12.	13.	14.
3	2	5	9	7	6	2	7
2	8	5	1	3	4	8	6
+7	+6	+6	+7	+4	+3	+4	+3

15.	16.	17.	18.	19.	20.	21.	22.
4	3	3	7	4	8	2	4
6	2	5	2	1	1	6	5
+8	+8	+8	+7	+6	+9	+5	+7

Mixed Applications

Library Books Borrowed				
Student	September	October	November	Total Number of Books
Rosa	4	3	5	
Jason	2	8	4	
Marco	5	1	6	

23. Find the total number of books each student borrowed. Complete the table.

24. In which month were most books borrowed?

_____

WRITER'S CORNER

25. Write a word problem using the information in the table titled Library Books Borrowed.

_____

_____

Estimating Sums

Estimate the sum by using front-end digits.

1. $5.23 + $2.78 = _____   2. 418 + 310 = _____   3. $7.03 + $1.64 = _____

Estimate the sum by using rounding.

4. $7.25 + $0.98 = _____   5. 362 + 194 = _____   6. 2,356 + 4,600 = _____

Estimate the sum.

7. $9.23
   + 1.85
   _____

8.   627
   +312
   _____

9. $8.04
   + 3.69
   _____

10.   764
   +149
   _____

11.   2,515
   +4,867
   _____

Mixed Applications

Estimate the sum.

12. The newsstand sold 48 magazines one day and 63 magazines the next. About how many magazines were sold?

_____

13. Janice delivers 55 newspapers on Saturday and 86 newspapers on Sunday. About how many newspapers does she deliver each weekend?

_____

EVERYDAY MATH CONNECTION

Estimate the total cost of the items on each grocery list.

14. milk
    bananas

_____

15. cereal
    can of soup

_____

16. meat
    bananas
    bread

_____

17. milk
    cereal
    bread
    can of soup

_____

PRICE LIST

$2.89 $7.29 $2.79 MILK $1.89 $1.29 BREAD SOUP $1.12

Problem Solving
Choose a Strategy

Choose a strategy. Solve.

1. Four students ran a race. Sally finished after Joe. Edith finished before Joe but after Gerry. Who finished last?

   _____

2. Ramón left his office and drove 15 miles to fix a broken cable. Then he drove in the same direction for 23 more miles. How far from the office was he?

   _____

3. Mrs. Wauneka can weave 12 shawls each month. It is now January 1. About how many shawls can she finish before the crafts show on May 5?

   _____

4. First 3 sunfish each ate 3 minnows. Then a bass ate all 3 sunfish and a trout. Last, a huge gar ate the bass and an eel. How many creatures were eaten?

   _____

GEOGRAPHY CONNECTION

The nature center at Park Resort is 2 km from the entrance. The lake is 4 km from the nature center along one road. The campground is 3 km from the nature center along another road. A 5-km road joins the lake and the campground.

5. On another piece of paper, draw a map of the resort.

6. Mr. DeVon drove from the entrance to the nature center and then to the campground. How far did he drive?

   _____

15

Adding Two-Digit Numbers

Find the sum. In Exercises 1–18, ring the columns in which you needed to regroup.

1. 46
  + 13

2. 16
  + 65

3. 27
  + 38

4. 67
  + 29

5. 68
  + 82

6. 57
  + 89

7. 95
  + 33

8. 28
  + 26

9. 29
  + 49

10. 87
  + 87

11. 33
  + 27

12. 91
  + 84

13. 84
  + 56

14. 23
  + 31

15. 73
  + 25

16. 57
  + 72

17. 97
  + 49

18. 43
  + 14

19. 67 + 96 = _____

20. 43 + 92 = _____

21. 37 + 98 = _____

22. 75 + 58 = _____

23. 25 + 91 = _____

24. 79 + 46 = _____

Mixed Applications

The table shows the number of seconds it took for each team to finish the race. Complete the table.

Race Times (in seconds)

	Team	Race 1	Race 2	Total
25.	Blue team	65	78	
26.	White team	83	95	
27.	Red team	64	82	
28.	Brown team	92	69	

29. Which team finished both races in the least time?

_____

30. Which team took the most time to finish both races?

_____

LOGICAL REASONING

Find the missing digits.

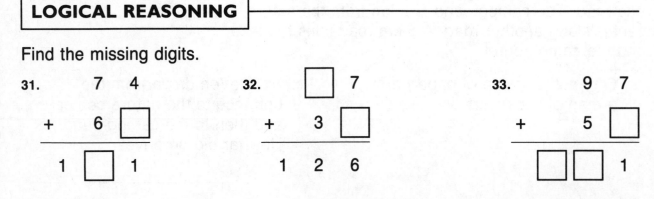

31.
  7 4
  + 6 ☐
  1 ☐ 1

32.
  ☐ 7
  + 3 ☐
  1 2 6

33.
  9 7
  + 5 ☐
  ☐ ☐ 1

Adding Three-Digit Numbers

Find the sum. Ring the columns in which you needed to regroup.

1.	348 +236	2.	374 +561	3.	733 +548	4.	971 +309	5.	150 +236
6.	895 +364	7.	584 +263	8.	475 +650	9.	692 +897	10.	234 +723
11.	165 +632	12.	242 +639	13.	760 +486	14.	365 +678	15.	173 +445
16.	$2.56 + 2.17	17.	$2.33 + 3.78	18.	$2.54 + 1.30	19.	$7.75 + 6.80	20.	$2.45 + 9.32

Mixed Applications

21. The Easton Art Club paid $784 for a new painting and $341 for a piece of sculpture. How much did the club pay for the two works?

22. The art show has 368 pieces of jewelry and 293 pieces of pottery. How many pieces of jewelry and pottery are in the show?

MIXED REVIEW

Estimate by rounding to the nearest ten or to the nearest ten cents.

1. 62 _____   2. 76 _____   3. 84 _____   4. 35 _____

5. $1.25 _____   6. $0.57 _____   7. $1.54 _____   8. $0.21 _____

Estimate by rounding to the nearest hundred or to the nearest dollar.

9. 568 _____   10. 372 _____   11. 633 _____   12. 921 _____

13. $4.75 _____   14. $6.25 _____   15. $8.39 _____   16. $7.58 _____

Adding Three or More Addends

Find the sum.

1.
```
   32
   40
 + 17
```

2.
```
   45
   33
 + 57
```

3.
```
  537
  624
 +769
```

4.
```
 6,904
   137
+3,264
```

5.
```
 2,408
    39
 +  359
```

6.
```
   15
   26
   48
 + 37
```

7.
```
    98
   346
   297
 +  16
```

8.
```
 $5.68
  3.27
  1.41
 + 0.84
```

9.
```
 $ 9.83
  37.64
   8.39
 +  1.72
```

10.
```
 $0.98
  3.46
  2.97
 + 0.49
```

Mixed Applications

11. It took Marc 25 minutes to wash his car, 18 minutes to vacuum it, and 90 minutes to wax it. How many minutes did he spend cleaning his car?

_____

12. Marc spent $3.89 for car wax, $1.55 for a sponge, and $2.19 for window cleaner. How much money did he spend?

_____

13. Use the table. Find how many cars were washed each month.

March _____

April _____

May _____

Ace Car Wax Business

Month	Number of Cars	
	Washed Only	Washed and Waxed
March	3,657	1,582
April	2,819	2,476
May	6,538	4,728

LOGICAL REASONING

Use the digits 1, 2, 2, 4, 5, 9.
Write a digit in each box to make

14. the least possible sum.

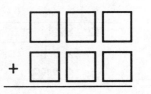

15. the greatest possible sum.

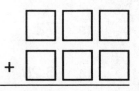

Estimating Differences

Estimate the difference by rounding.

1. 935 − 265	2. 728 − 333	3. 566 − 247	4. 641 − 258	5. 932 − 567
6. 4,731 − 1,545	7. 9,632 − 5,738	8. 7,092 − 4,666	9. $22.97 − 13.36	10. $63.75 − 37.32

11. 625 − 367 = _____

12. 800 − 339 = _____

13. $71.72 − $9.98 = _____

14. 8,157 − 4,461 = _____

Mixed Applications

15. There are 748 kinds of animals in the zoo. Wild Animal Park has 293 kinds. About how many more kinds of animals are there in the zoo than in Wild Animal Park?

   _____

16. The reptile house at the zoo had 432 reptiles. Last week 185 of the reptiles were moved to another zoo. Were there *more than* or *fewer than* 200 reptiles remaining in the reptile house?

   _____

NUMBER SENSE

Use estimation to help you ring the weight that will balance the scale.

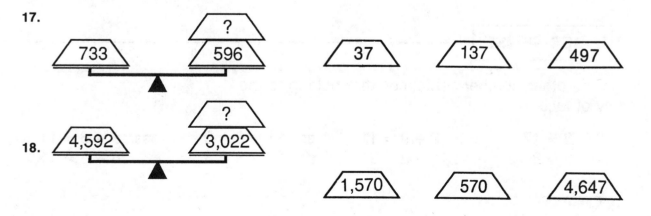

17.

733   596   ?   37   137   497

18.

4,592   3,022   ?   1,570   570   4,647

Subtracting Two-Digit Numbers

Find the difference. Ring the columns in Exercises 1–18
in which you needed to regroup.

1. 79
    − 25

2. 95
    − 58

3. 87
    − 76

4. 73
    − 56

5. 43
    − 39

6. 98
    − 67

7. 80
    − 29

8. 76
    − 27

9. 42
    − 3

10. 25
    − 15

11. 76
    − 34

12. 61
    − 26

13. 51
    − 49

14. 59
    − 35

15. 84
    − 39

16. 65
    − 46

17. 47
    − 15

18. 80
    − 60

19. 53 − 45 = _____

20. 81 − 63 = _____

21. 78 − 52 = _____

22. 92 − 84 = _____

23. 93 − 37 = _____

24. 67 − 42 = _____

25. 45 − 32 = _____

26. 68 − 49 = _____

27. 80 − 29 = _____

Mixed Applications

28. Harrison's Hardware Store received a shipment of 85 garden hoses. The store sold 18 of the hoses. How many garden hoses did the store have left?

_____

29. Mr. Harrison had 54 snow shovels in his store. After a sale, 8 shovels were left. How many shovels did Mr. Harrison sell?

_____

NUMBER SENSE

Write the other number sentences that belong to the
family of facts.

30. 9 + 8 = 17
    17 − 9 = 8

31. 2 + 9 = 11
    11 − 2 = 9

32. 11 − 8 = 3
    11 − 3 = 8

33. 5 + 6 = 11
    6 + 5 = 11

_____   _____   _____   _____

_____   _____   _____   _____

Subtracting Three-Digit Numbers

Find the difference.

1. 517
    − 292

2. 789
    − 294

3. 793
    − 189

4. 747
    − 628

5. 641
    − 250

6. $8.37
    − 1.57

7. $6.35
    − 2.27

8. $7.26
    − 1.58

9. $6.42
    − 0.88

10. $4.55
    − 3.96

11. 806 − 257 = _____

12. 912 − 88 = _____

13. $6.34 − $5.58 = _____

14. $9.53 − $6.59 = _____

Mixed Applications

The table shows the quantity of fish Emilio's Fish Market received on Saturday. Use the table to answer the questions.

Saturday's Shipment	
Type of Fish	**Weight in Kilograms**
Trout	334
Whitefish	187
Flounder	435
Salmon	282
Sole	195

15. How much more trout than sole did the market receive?

_____

16. How many kilograms of fish did Emilio receive on Saturday?

_____

VISUAL THINKING

17. Choose the model that shows how you would regroup to solve the number sentence.

    252 − 37 = ☐

    a.   b.   c.

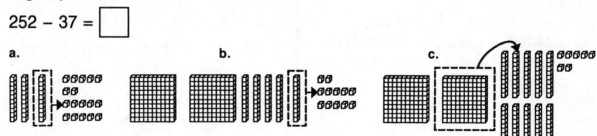

21

Problem-Solving Strategy
Make a Table

The table shows the after-school workshop schedule.
Use the table to answer the questions.

After-School Workshop Schedule		
Class	Day	Time
Cooking	Mon. or Fri.	3:30–4:30
Stamp Collecting	Tues. only	4:30–5:15
Computers	Tues. only	4:30–5:30
Gymnastics	Wed. or Thurs.	4:00–5:00
Ceramics	Mon. or Thurs.	3:30–4:15

1. What three things can you learn from reading the table?

   _____

   _____

2. What classes could you take on a Thursday?

   _____

3. Explain why you could not take both stamp collecting and computers.

   _____

 **Mixed Applications** **STRATEGIES**
- Draw a Picture
- Make a Table
- Write a Number Sentence
- Find a Pattern

Choose a strategy and solve.

4. On Thursday, 24 students signed up for the ceramics class. On Friday, 9 more signed up, and 3 dropped the class. How many students are in the class?

   _____

5. Ted leaves school and drives north for 42 km. He turns around and drives south for 19 km. Then he stops to make a phone call. How far from school is he?

   _____

WRITER'S CORNER

6. Make a table that shows a schedule for an after-school sports workshop. Include the sport, the teacher, and the location of the class. Write three questions that can be answered by using the table.

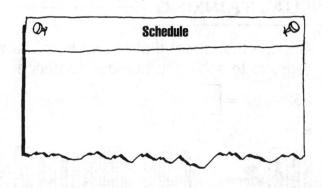

   _____

   _____

Exploring Subtraction and Money

Write each problem in expanded notation. Then find the difference.

1. $9.00
   − 3.45   _____

2. $48.01
   − 29.34   _____

3. $24.36
   − 9.57   _____

Choose the correct number sentence. Then solve.

4. Paco spent $46.85 on a new winter jacket. He gave the salesclerk $50.00. How much change did Paco get?

   a. $46.85 + $50.00 = ☐

   b. $50.00 + $46.85 = ☐

   c. $50.00 − $46.85 = ☐

   _____

5. Mrs. Chow paid the cleaners $27.35 to clean a rug. She paid $12.86 to have her draperies cleaned. How much did she spend?

   a. $27.35 − $12.86 = ☐

   b. $27.35 + $12.86 = ☐

   c. $27.35 + ☐ = $12.86

   _____

EVERYDAY MATH CONNECTION

6. Tyrone has $3.00. He wants to buy a package of stickers for $0.65 and a sticker book for $1.25. Does he have enough money?

   _____

7. Mr. Jones wants to buy a notebook for $0.55, a pen for $0.90, and a ruler for $0.85. Mr. Jones has $2.50. Does he have enough money?

   _____

Add and Subtract with Greater Numbers

First, estimate the sum or difference. Then, use a calculator or pencil and paper to find the exact answer.

1. 4,731
  − 1,545
	2. 5,789
	  + 1,861
		3. 9,632
		  − 5,768
			4. 3,569
			  + 4,483
				5. 7,092
				  − 4,666

6. 2,739
  + 1,985
	7. 6,744
	  − 1,375
		8. 5,837
		  − 2,678
			9. 7,458
			  + 3,749
				10. 6,832
				  + 2,818

11. 8,549 − 7,234 = _____

12. 4,960 − 3,879 = _____

13. 6,707 + 5,499 = _____

14. 43,476 − 30,908 = _____

Mixed Applications

The table shows some readings on the electric meter at the Santa Fe Restaurant.

15. Complete the table. The amount used is the difference between the new reading and the last reading.

16. What was the total number of kilowatt-hours used?

_____

Number of Kilowatt-Hours			
	New Reading	Last Reading	Amount Used
April	5,256	4,937	
May	8,107	5,256	
June	11,009	8,107	
July	12,142	11,009	

| **MIXED REVIEW** |

Compare. Write <, >, or = for ◯.

1. 142 ◯ 84   2. 52 ◯ 252   3. 684 ◯ 684

Find the sum or difference.

4. 14 + 76 + 30 + 41 = _____   5. 743 − 159 = _____

Exploring Multiplication and Division

Write the multiplication number sentence for each array.

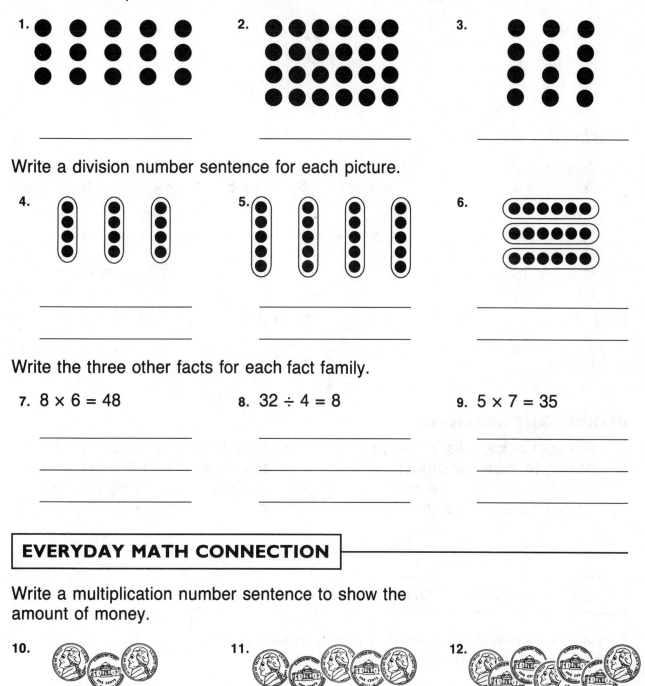

1.

2.

3.

_____

_____

_____

Write a division number sentence for each picture.

4.

5.

6.

_____

_____

_____

_____

_____

_____

Write the three other facts for each fact family.

7. $8 \times 6 = 48$

8. $32 \div 4 = 8$

9. $5 \times 7 = 35$

_____

_____

_____

_____

_____

_____

_____

_____

_____

EVERYDAY MATH CONNECTION

Write a multiplication number sentence to show the amount of money.

10.

11.

12.

_____

_____

_____

Multiplication
2 and 3 as Factors

Draw an array to solve.

1. $2 \times 6 =$ _____
2. $3 \times 8 =$ _____
3. $2 \times 7 =$ _____

Find the product.

4.	5.	6.	7.	8.	9.	10.	11.	12.
2	2	3	2	3	3	2	2	2
$\times 1$	$\times 4$	$\times 1$	$\times 8$	$\times 6$	$\times 8$	$\times 9$	$\times 5$	$\times 6$

13.	14.	15.	16.	17.	18.	19.	20.	21.
3	2	2	3	2	3	3	3	3
$\times 9$	$\times 7$	$\times 2$	$\times 4$	$\times 3$	$\times 5$	$\times 2$	$\times 7$	$\times 3$

22. $8 \times 3 =$ _____
23. $5 \times 3 =$ _____
24. $6 \times 2 =$ _____
25. $9 \times 2 =$ _____

26. $4 \times 2 =$ _____
27. $7 \times 3 =$ _____
28. $1 \times 3 =$ _____
29. $8 \times 2 =$ _____

Mixed Applications

30. The post office sells 2 special stamps in each package. Mike buys 5 packages. How many stamps does Mike buy?

31. Mike buys stamps for $1.45, envelopes for $1.20, and a mailing carton for $0.75. How much does he pay?

SPORTS CONNECTION

A touchdown in football is worth 6 points. A field goal is worth 3 points. How many points are scored for

32. 2 touchdowns and 5 field goals? _____

33. 3 touchdowns and 3 field goals? _____

34. 4 touchdowns and 2 field goals? _____

Multiplication
4 and 5 as Factors

Draw an array for each multiplication sentence.

1. $4 \times 5 = 20$ 2. $5 \times 9 = 45$ 3. $5 \times 8 = 40$

Find the product.

4. 5 $\times 3$	5. 5 $\times 5$	6. 4 $\times 1$	7. 5 $\times 2$	8. 4 $\times 6$	9. 5 $\times 6$	10. 4 $\times 3$	11. 5 $\times 7$	12. 4 $\times 8$

13. 4 $\times 4$	14. 5 $\times 4$	15. 4 $\times 7$	16. 5 $\times 9$	17. 4 $\times 2$	18. 5 $\times 1$	19. 4 $\times 5$	20. 5 $\times 8$	21. 4 $\times 9$

22. $5 \times 8 = $ _____   23. $5 \times 3 = $ _____   24. $5 \times 7 = $ _____   25. $9 \times 5 = $ _____

26. $5 \times 4 = $ _____   27. $4 \times 7 = $ _____   28. $4 \times 4 = $ _____   29. $8 \times 4 = $ _____

Mixed Applications

30. There are 6 helicopters at the airport. Each helicopter can hold 5 people. How many people can all the helicopters hold?

_____

31. Company A owns 5 helicopters. It buys 7 new helicopters. How many helicopters does Company A have now?

_____

NUMBER SENSE

Compare. Write $<$, $>$, or $=$.

32. $4 \times 2 \bigcirc 9$ 33. $7 \times 3 \bigcirc 20$ 34. $6 \times 2 \bigcirc 12$

35. $25 \bigcirc 8 \times 3$ 36. $6 \times 3 \bigcirc 9 \times 2$ 37. $5 \times 3 \bigcirc 8 \times 2$

Mental Math
Using Multiplication Properties

Write **a, b, c,** or **d** to tell which property is shown.

a. Order Property	b. Property of One	c. Zero Property	d. Grouping Property

1. $5 \times 1 = 5$ _____

2. $8 \times 0 = 0$ _____

3. $2 \times (4 \times 1) = (2 \times 4) \times 1$ _____

4. $3 \times 4 = 4 \times 3$ ___

5. $1 \times 9 = 9 \times 1$ ___

6. $7 \times (3 \times 2) = (7 \times 3) \times 2$ _____

Use the multiplication properties to solve.

7. $5 \times 7 = 35$

   $7 \times 5 =$ _____

8. $9 \times 4 = 36$

   $4 \times 9 =$ _____

9. $3 \times 6 = 18$

   $6 \times 3 =$ _____

10. $8 \times 2 = 16$

    $2 \times 8 =$ _____

11. $8 \times 0 =$ _____

12. $0 \times 7 =$ _____

13. $1 \times 4 =$ _____

14. $4 \times (3 \times 2) =$ _____

15. $2 \times (1 \times 9) =$ _____

16. $3 \times (84 \times 0) =$ _____

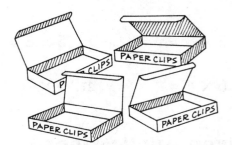

Mixed Applications

17. Beth wants to clip her reports together. She finds 4 boxes of paper clips to use.

    a. She opens the boxes. All of the boxes are empty. Write a number sentence that tells the number of paper clips she has.

    _____

    b. Beth puts 1 paper clip into each of the 4 boxes. Write a number sentence that tells the number of paper clips in all.

    _____

VISUAL THINKING

18. Circle the letters of the two arrays which show that $3 \times 5 = 5 \times 3$.

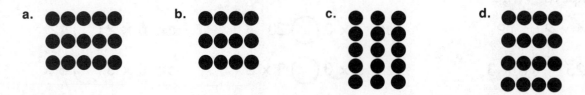

a.   b.   c.   d.

Problem Solving
Too Much or Too Little Information

If the problem has too little information, write what fact is missing. If the problem has too much information, tell which fact is not needed. Solve the problem if you can.

1. When the bike-a-thon was over, the children were taken to Frank's Pizza. Each child ordered 2 slices of pizza. How many slices were ordered?

_____

_____

2. Eddie wanted to buy a new helmet to wear during the bike-a-thon. The helmet cost $24.95. It is on sale for $19.95. Eddie had $18.90. How much more did Eddie need to buy the helmet?

_____

_____

Mixed Applications > **STRATEGIES** • Find a Pattern • Make a Table • Draw a Picture

Choose a strategy and solve.

3. Tina crochets a quilt. It has a red stripe, then a blue stripe, and then a white stripe. This pattern repeats itself. What color is the eighth stripe?

_____

4. Jay is younger than Bruce. Fran is older than Bruce. Anne's age is between Bruce's age and Fran's age. Which person is the youngest?

_____

WRITER'S CORNER

5. Write the facts that you see in the drawing.

_____

_____

6. Write one problem that can be answered using the facts.

_____

_____

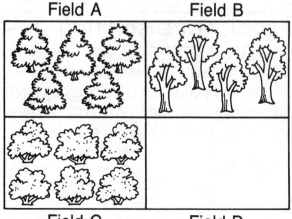

Field A   Field B

Field C   Field D

Multiplication
6 and 7 as Factors

Draw an array to solve.

1. $6 \times 7 =$ _____   2. $7 \times 4 =$ _____   3. $6 \times 9 =$ _____

Find the product.

4. $\begin{array}{r} 7 \\ \times 6 \\ \hline \end{array}$ 5. $\begin{array}{r} 6 \\ \times 1 \\ \hline \end{array}$ 6. $\begin{array}{r} 7 \\ \times 1 \\ \hline \end{array}$ 7. $\begin{array}{r} 6 \\ \times 7 \\ \hline \end{array}$ 8. $\begin{array}{r} 7 \\ \times 2 \\ \hline \end{array}$ 9. $\begin{array}{r} 7 \\ \times 4 \\ \hline \end{array}$ 10. $\begin{array}{r} 6 \\ \times 3 \\ \hline \end{array}$ 11. $\begin{array}{r} 7 \\ \times 7 \\ \hline \end{array}$ 12. $\begin{array}{r} 6 \\ \times 6 \\ \hline \end{array}$

13. $6 \times 8 =$ _____   14. $8 \times 7 =$ _____   15. $9 \times 6 =$ _____   16. $2 \times 7 =$ _____

17. $6 \times 6 =$ _____   18. $7 \times 3 =$ _____   19. $6 \times 9 =$ _____   20. $5 \times 6 =$ _____

Mixed Applications

21. Employees at the music store put new strings on 7 violins. Each violin gets 4 strings. How many strings are used?

    _____

22. The Wilson School has 7 pianos. If 2 of the pianos need repair, how many pianos are in working order?

    _____

LOGICAL REASONING

23. Complete the multiplication wheel. Multiply the center number by each number around it. When the answer is given, find the missing factor.

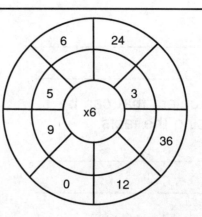

Multiplication
8 and 9 as Factors

Draw an array to solve.

1. 4 × 8 = _____   2. 3 × 9 = _____   3. 8 × 8 = _____

Find the product.

4.	9	5.	8	6.	9	7.	8	8.	9	9.	8	10.	9	11.	8	12.	8
	×8		×3		×1		×7		×2		×1		×7		×4		×9

13.	8	14.	9	15.	8	16.	9	17.	8	18.	9	19.	9	20.	9	21.	8
	×8		×6		×2		×5		×6		×9		×3		×4		×5

Mixed Applications

22. A baker can make 8 batches of muffins each hour. How many batches can the baker make in 7 hours?

_____

23. The baker has 8 rows of muffins on a baking sheet. There are 6 muffins in each row. How many muffins are there?

_____

VISUAL THINKING

24. Ring the letter of the correct number sentence to help you find the number of rolls on the baking sheet. Then solve.

a. 4 × 4 = ?

b. (4 × 4) − 2 = ?

c. (4 × 4) + 2 = ?

_____ rolls

Mental Math
Practicing Multiplication Facts

Find the product.

1. 8 ×3	2. 9 ×6	3. 8 ×4	4. 3 ×6	5. 7 ×8	6. 5 ×4	7. 6 ×0	8. 4 ×4	9. 8 ×9
10. 4 ×6	11. 7 ×5	12. 9 ×9	13. 4 ×7	14. 5 ×6	15. 9 ×7	16. 4 ×4	17. 0 ×8	18. 7 ×6

Find the product.

19. $8 \times 8 =$ _____   20. $7 \times 3 =$ _____   21. $8 \times 6 =$ _____   22. $7 \times 7 =$ _____

23. $6 \times 1 =$ _____   24. $4 \times 9 =$ _____   25. $9 \times 0 =$ _____   26. $5 \times 9 =$ _____

Complete each multiplication table.

27.

×	0	1	2	3	4	5	6	7	8	9
8	0	8	16							

28.

×	0	1	2	3	4	5	6	7	8	9
7	0	7	14							

Mixed Applications

29. There are 6 ears of yellow corn and 2 ears of white corn in each bag. There are 8 bags. How many ears of corn are there?

_____

30. The grocer puts 3 green peppers in each of 8 packages. He puts 5 green peppers in the ninth package. How many green peppers does the grocer have?

_____

MIXED REVIEW

Find the sum or difference.

1. $63.75 + 7.39	2. $54.85 − 18.67	3. $18.05 + 26.76	4. $88.72 − 29.63	5. $25.44 − 8.78

Connecting Multiplication and Division

Write a multiplication number sentence and a division number sentence for each picture.

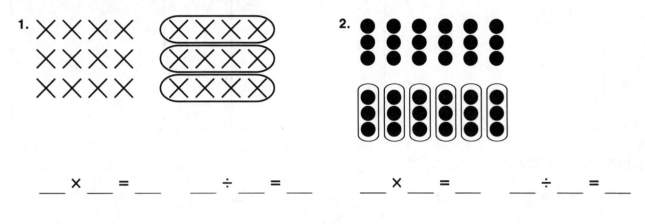

___ × ___ = ___   ___ ÷ ___ = ___   ___ × ___ = ___   ___ ÷ ___ = ___

Complete. Write a number sentence to show the inverse operation.

3. $36 \div 4 =$ _____

_____

4. $5 \times$ _____ $= 35$

_____

5. _____ $\times 9 = 72$

_____

Find the missing factor.

6. _____ $\times 2 = 10$

7. $1 \times$ _____ $= 9$

8. _____ $\times 3 = 21$

Mixed Applications

Ring the letter of the correct number sentence. Solve.

9. Mrs. Panko has 18 tulip bulbs. She plants 2 tulip bulbs in each flowerpot. How many pots does she use?

a. $18 \times 2 = \square$ b. $18 \div 2 = \square$

_____

NUMBER SENSE

Complete. Use *doubles* to help you multiply.

10. 4 fours = 16

So, 8 fours = ____ .

11. 4 nines = 36

So, 8 nines = ____ .

12. 3 sixes = 18

So, 6 sixes = ____ .

Dividing by 2 and 3

Draw a picture to solve.

1. $9 \div 3 =$ _____

2. $12 \div 2 =$ _____

3. $18 \div 2 =$ _____

Find the quotient.

4. $27 \div 3 =$ _____

5. $3 \div 3 =$ _____

6. $18 \div 3 =$ _____

7. $4 \div 2 =$ _____

8. $8 \div 2 =$ _____

9. $21 \div 3 =$ _____

10. $14 \div 2 =$ _____

11. $15 \div 3 =$ _____

12. $2\overline{)16}$

13. $3\overline{)6}$

14. $3\overline{)27}$

15. $3\overline{)24}$

16. $2\overline{)4}$

17. $3\overline{)15}$

18. $3\overline{)24}$

19. $2\overline{)6}$

20. $2\overline{)10}$

21. $3\overline{)18}$

22. $3\overline{)12}$

23. $2\overline{)2}$

Mixed Applications

24. The pet shop has 16 puppies. Store employees put 2 puppies in each cage. How many cages are used?

_____

25. The pet shop has 24 bags of dog food. If 3 bags are used each day, for how many days will the dog food last?

_____

VISUAL THINKING

Draw a picture of the quotient.

26.

27.

28.

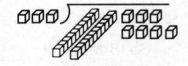

34

Dividing by 4 and 5

Draw a picture to solve.

1. 30 ÷ 6 = _____

2. 20 ÷ 4 = _____

3. 25 ÷ 5 = _____

Find the quotient.

4. 40 ÷ 5 = _____   5. 28 ÷ 4 = _____   6. 15 ÷ 5 = _____   7. 32 ÷ 4 = _____

8. 35 ÷ 5 = _____   9. 16 ÷ 4 = _____   10. 36 ÷ 4 = _____   11. 5 ÷ 5 = _____

12. 4)‾20   13. 5)‾25   14. 4)‾12   15. 5)‾30   16. 5)‾45   17. 4)‾8

Mixed Applications

18. Mrs. Thomas has 45 reading books in her classroom. Each bookshelf will hold 9 books. How many bookshelves are needed to hold all the reading books?

19. Mr. Dalton spent $46.85 on a new calculator for the science teacher. He gave the sales clerk $50.00. How much change did he get?

LOGICAL REASONING

Find the missing factors to complete each table.

20.

Multiply by 4	
Input	Output
☐	20
☐	36

21.

Multiply by 5	
Input	Output
☐	15
☐	45

22.

Multiply by ☐	
Input	Output
2	16
4	32

Problem Solving
Choose a Strategy

Mixed Applications >	STRATEGIES	• Make a Table to Analyze Data • Find a Pattern • Draw a Picture

Choose a strategy and solve.

1. The farmer has 72 chickens. There are 9 chickens in each cage. How many cages of chickens does the farmer have?

_____

2. The farmer uses 2 bags of feed each day. How many bags of feed does the farmer need for one week?

_____

3. Bert, Amy, Della, and Sophia stood in line to get their paychecks. Bert stood behind Sophia. Sophia stood behind Amy. Della was last in line. Who was third in line?

_____

4. Della exercised a pony for 15 minutes on the first day. The second day she exercised the pony for 20 minutes. The third day she did 25 minutes, and so on. At this rate of increase, how many minutes of exercise was the pony getting on the seventh day?

_____

VISUAL THINKING

Write a multiplication number sentence to tell how many.

5. How many 🌳 ? _____

6. How many 🚪 ? _____

7. How many 🪟 ? _____

8. How many ▯ ? _____

Division with Zero and One

Find the quotient.

1. $0 \div 7 =$ _____
2. $3 \div 3 =$ _____
3. $9 \div 9 =$ _____
4. $0 \div 4 =$ _____

5. $18 \div 1 =$ _____
6. $5 \div 5 =$ _____
7. $64 \div 1 =$ _____
8. $7 \div 1 =$ _____

9. $0 \div 15 =$ _____
10. $8 \div 8 =$ _____
11. $17 \div 1 =$ _____
12. $0 \div 6 =$ _____

13. $4\overline{)4}$
14. $2\overline{)0}$
15. $7\overline{)7}$
16. $1\overline{)3}$
17. $1\overline{)1}$
18. $6\overline{)6}$

19. $9\overline{)0}$
20. $5\overline{)5}$
21. $1\overline{)24}$
22. $1\overline{)8}$
23. $14\overline{)0}$
24. $8\overline{)8}$

Mixed Applications

Use the table to answer Exercises 25–27.

25. For how many hours does Ben work each week?

_____

26. Who works the same number of hours as Martha?

_____

27. If Cho earns $35 each week, how much is he paid per hour?

_____

Part-time Help Schedule							
	Number of Hours Each Day						
Name	S	M	T	W	Th	F	S
Martha	3		3		3		
Ben	2	2	2	2	2	2	2
Eli	4						4
Whitney	2		2		2		2
Rámon		3		3		3	
Cho		1	1	1	1	1	
Peg	6						6

NUMBER SENSE

Compare. Write $<$, $>$, or $=$.

28. $46 \div 1 \bigcirc 1 \times 46$
29. $18 \div 1 \bigcirc 28 \div 1$

30. $0 \div 30 \bigcirc 0 \div 49$
31. $4 \times 5 \bigcirc 20 \div 1$

Dividing by 6 and 7

Draw a picture to solve.

1. 35 ÷ 7 = _____

2. 36 ÷ 6 = _____

3. 21 ÷ 7 = _____

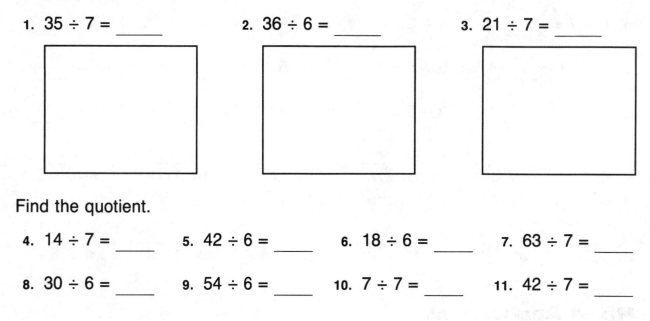

Find the quotient.

4. 14 ÷ 7 = _____

5. 42 ÷ 6 = _____

6. 18 ÷ 6 = _____

7. 63 ÷ 7 = _____

8. 30 ÷ 6 = _____

9. 54 ÷ 6 = _____

10. 7 ÷ 7 = _____

11. 42 ÷ 7 = _____

12. $6\overline{)24}$

13. $7\overline{)28}$

14. $6\overline{)12}$

15. $7\overline{)49}$

16. $6\overline{)6}$

17. $7\overline{)56}$

Mixed Applications

18. Jason earns $63 each day as a ticket agent. He usually works 7 hours each day. Last Sunday he worked only 5 hours. How much money did he earn last Sunday?

19. The express train makes 24 trips each day. The train runs for 6 hours. It makes the same number of trips each hour. How many trips does the train make each hour?

LOGICAL REASONING

Write whether you divide to find *how many groups* or *how many in each group*. Solve.

20. The gas station puts 24 new tires on 6 cars. Each car gets the same number of tires. How many tires does each car get?

21. Mr. Feldman has 40 new car mirrors. There are 5 mirrors in each box. How many boxes of mirrors are there?

Dividing by 8 and 9

Draw a picture to solve.

1. 36 ÷ 9 = _____

2. 40 ÷ 8 = _____

3. 27 ÷ 9 = _____

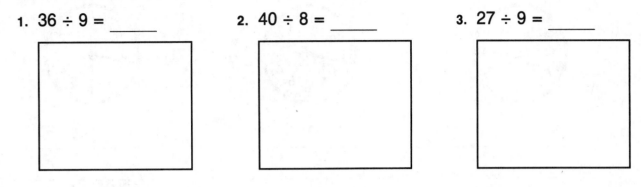

Find the quotient.

4. 56 ÷ 8 = _____

5. 18 ÷ 9 = _____

6. 24 ÷ 8 = _____

7. 63 ÷ 9 = _____

8. 32 ÷ 8 = _____

9. 8 ÷ 8 = _____

10. 45 ÷ 9 = _____

11. 72 ÷ 8 = _____

12. $9\overline{)54}$

13. $8\overline{)64}$

14. $8\overline{)48}$

15. $9\overline{)72}$

16. $9\overline{)9}$

17. $8\overline{)16}$

18. $9\overline{)81}$

19. $9\overline{)27}$

20. $8\overline{)24}$

21. $8\overline{)56}$

22. $9\overline{)18}$

23. $8\overline{)32}$

Mixed Applications

24. The florist uses 56 roses to make 8 bouquets. The same number of roses are in each bouquet. How many roses are in each bouquet?

_____

25. Ms. Cohen makes 6 baskets of flowers for a party. She uses 9 flowers in each basket. How many flowers does she use?

_____

MIXED REVIEW

Write the three other facts for each fact family.

1. 9 × 5 = 45

2. 48 ÷ 6 = 8

3. 8 × 9 = 72

_____

_____

_____

Telling Time

Write the time in two different ways.

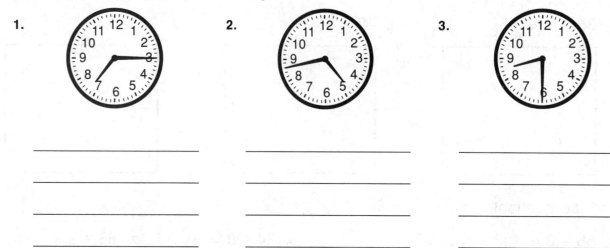

1.

2.

3.

_____

_____

_____

_____

_____

_____

_____

_____

_____

Match the time with the clock.

4. four minutes past six

5. twenty-three minutes to eight

$$\boxed{6:04}$$

$$\boxed{7:37}$$

Mixed Applications

6. It took 14 minutes for Suki to prepare the muffin batter and 22 minutes to bake the muffins. How many minutes did it take her to make the muffins?

_____

7. Jim preheated the oven at 3:00. Jason prepared the bread dough at 2:50. Helen put some rolls in the oven at a quarter past three. Which activity took place first?

_____

LOGICAL REASONING

Underline the time that fits both clues.

8.
- It is given in quarter hours.
- It is earlier than half past six.

a. four-ten

b. five-thirty

c. six forty-five

Time

A.M. and P.M.

Write the time by using numbers and A.M. or P.M.

1. The sun rises.

_____

2. The gas station closes.

3. Maria eats lunch.

_____

4. the time you start school

_____

5. the time you eat dinner

_____

Mixed Applications

6. A movie on whales was scheduled for noon. A movie on dolphins was scheduled for two-twenty. Which show came first?

_____

7. The class saw a film about sharks at fifteen minutes before eleven. Write the time using A.M. or P.M.

_____

| EVERYDAY MATH CONNECTION |

For some jobs, workers "punch" a time card to keep a record of the hours worked. Use the time card to answer Exercises 8–9.

8. When did Roberto leave work for the day on Wednesday?

_____

9. When did Roberto return to work from lunch on Tuesday?

_____

Week Ending *11-5*				
Name *Roberto Suarez*				
	In	Out	In	Out
Mon	8:30	11:30	12:30	4:30
Tue	9:00	12:00	1:00	5:00
Wed	8:00	11:00	1:00	6:00
Thu				
Fri				
Sat				
Sun				

Time
Estimation

Choose the most reasonable unit of time for each
(sec, min, hr, d, wk, mo, yr).

1. Summer lasts about 3 _____ .

2. It takes about 10 _____ to take a shower.

3. To eat your lunch takes about 20 _____ .

4. It takes about one _____ to snap your fingers.

Choose the best estimate for each.

5. The time it takes to eat dinner.

   a. 30 minutes

   b. 30 hours

   c. 3 days

6. The time it takes to get a good night's sleep.

   a. 8 seconds

   b. 80 minutes

   c. 8 hours

Mixed Applications

7. Jeff thought his piano lesson would last about one hour. His lesson started at 2:55 P.M. About what time will his lesson be over?

_____

8. Alice practiced playing the violin for 15 minutes. Then she practiced playing the piano for 35 minutes. Did her practicing last more or less than 1 hour?

_____

LOGICAL REASONING

9. Draw the hands on the last two clocks to complete the pattern.

Exploring Elapsed Time

Tell how much time has elapsed.

1.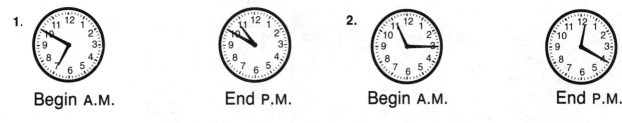

Begin A.M.   End P.M.   2.   Begin A.M.   End P.M.

_____   _____

Use the clocks to help you answer Exercises 3–5.

3. How many minutes pass from 1:20 P.M. to 1:55 P.M.?

_____

4. How many hours pass from 9:00 A.M. to 2:00 P.M.?

_____

5. What is the time when it is 30 minutes before 8:15 A.M.?

_____

Mixed Applications

6. Luis went outside to ride his bike at 3:35 P.M. His mother told him to be home by 4:10 P.M. How long did Luis have to ride his bike?

_____

7. Mr. Baxter wants to leave his house at 8:00 in the morning. He needs 50 minutes to get ready. What time should he get up?

_____

SCIENCE CONNECTION

8. Brenda works at a hospital. She takes blood samples from a patient every 45 minutes. She takes the first sample at 10:15 A.M. and the last sample at 1:15 P.M. Write in each time Brenda took a sample.

First Sample   Second Sample   Third Sample   Fourth Sample   Last Sample

_____   _____   _____   _____   _____

The Calendar

Use the calendar to answer Exercises 1–3.

October

Sun	Mon	Tues	Wed	Thurs	Fri	Sat
		1	2	3	4	5
6	7	8	9	10	11	12
13	14	15	16	17	18	19
20	21	22	23	24	25	26
27	28	29	30	31		

1. Write the date of the first Sunday during the festival. _____

2. How many days will the balloon festival last? _____

3. Write the date one week before the balloon festival begins. _____

Mixed Applications

Write the day and date. Use the October calendar.

4. 4 days after October 21

_____

5. The third Friday in October

_____

Solve.

6. John left for the balloon festival on Friday, October 11. Lisa left 3 days later. On what day and date did Lisa leave?

_____

7. Lisa bought a balloon festival T-shirt for $14.79. She gave the clerk $20.00. How much change should Lisa get?

_____

EVERYDAY MATH CONNECTION

Here is a date written in numerical form.

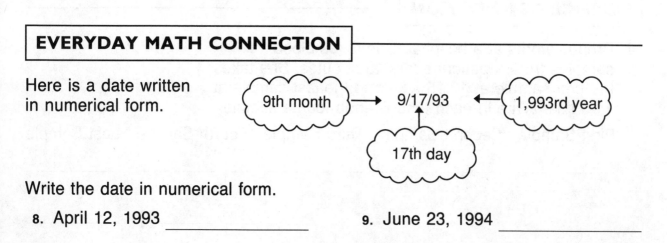

9th month → 9/17/93 ← 1,993rd year

17th day

Write the date in numerical form.

8. April 12, 1993 _____

9. June 23, 1994 _____

44

Problem Solving
Use a Table or a Schedule

Use the train schedule to answer Exercises 1–4.

1. Which train arrives in Linden at 10:05 A.M.?

_____

Train Schedule for Weekdays			
Station	Train A A.M.	Train B A.M.	Train C P.M.
Edison	7:12	9:00	12:10
Sunset	7:27	9:15	12:25
Fairfax	7:52	———	12:50
Woodruff	———	9:47	1:02
Linden	8:18	10:05	1:20
Layton	8:51	10:38	1:53

2. Which train arrives in Layton before 9:00 A.M.?

_____

3. How many trains stop in the morning at Fairfax?

_____

4. How long does it take Train A to go from Edison to Sunset?

_____

Mixed Applications > **STRATEGIES** • Find a Pattern • Draw a Picture • Write a Number Sentence

5. Train D stops every 20 minutes. The first stop is in Landville at 9:00 A.M. What time is it when the train makes its seventh stop in the town of Delray?

_____

6. A ticket for a trip from Wayne to Centerville costs $24.50. A ticket for a trip from Ardmore to Beltsville costs $18.75. Find the difference between the cost of the two tickets.

_____

SPORTS CONNECTION

Recorded times for many athletic events include seconds.

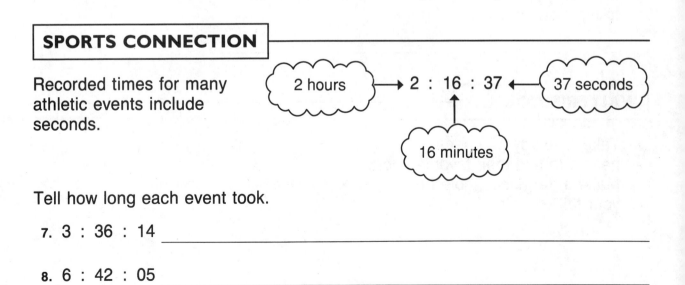

Tell how long each event took.

7. 3 : 36 : 14 _____

8. 6 : 42 : 05 _____

Collecting Data

Use this tally table to answer Exercises 1-4.

1. Which sport is the most popular?

   _____

2. How many people like basketball or football?

   _____

3. How many people participated in this survey? _____

4. Complete the frequency column.

Favorite Sports		
Sport	Tally	Frequency
Bowling	⊞ I	
Tennis	IIII	
Swimming	⊞ III	
Basketball	⊞ ⊞ ⊞	
Football	⊞ IIII	

Mixed Applications

Use the frequency table to answer Exercises 5-7.

5. How many more visitors attended Game 3 than Game 4?

   _____

6. To which game did the least number of visitors come?

   _____

Center School Soccer Team Number of Visitors at Home Games	
Game	Frequency
Game 1	140
Game 2	195
Game 3	182
Game 4	108
Game 5	220

7. List the games in order from greatest attendance to least attendance.

   _____

WRITER'S CORNER

8. Take a survey of at least ten people to find their favorite sport. Make a frequency table from your tallies.

Pictographs

Use the pictograph to answer Exercises 1–3.

Number of Shirts Sold	
Monday	👕 👕 👕 👕 👕 👕
Tuesday	👕 👕 👕 👕
Wednesday	👕 👕
Thursday	👕 👕 👕 👕
Friday	👕 👕 👕 👕 👕 👕 👕 👕
	Key: Each 👕 stands for 10 shirts.

1. On which day were fewest shirts sold? _____

2. Were more shirts sold on Tuesday or Wednesday? _____

3. How many shirts were sold on Wednesday? ___ Friday? ___ Monday? ___

Mixed Applications

Use the pictograph to answer Exercises 4–5. If you cannot solve, explain why.

Boxes of Buttons Used	
Monday	⊚ ⊚ ⊚ ⊚ ⊚ ⊚ ⊚
Tuesday	⊚ ⊚ ⊚ ⊚
Wednesday	⊚ ⊚
Thursday	⊚ ⊚ ⊚
Friday	⊚ ⊚ ⊚ ⊚ ⊚
	Key: Each ⊚ stands for 20 boxes of buttons.

4. How many more boxes of buttons were used on Monday than on Thursday?

_____

5. The shirt factory pays $0.09 for each button. How much did they spend on buttons on Monday?

_____

VISUAL THINKING

If ⊚ stands for 20 boxes of buttons, then ◖ stands for 10 boxes of buttons.

Think: $\frac{1}{2}$ of 20 is 10.

Tell the number of boxes of buttons used.

6. ⊚ ⊚ ⊚ ◖ _____

7. ⊚ ⊚ ◖ _____

8. ⊚ ⊚ ⊚ ⊚ ⊚ ⊚ ⊚ ◖ _____

Bar Graphs

The art teacher asked students which art project they
want to work on. A bar graph shows the results. Use
this graph to answer Exercises 1–5.

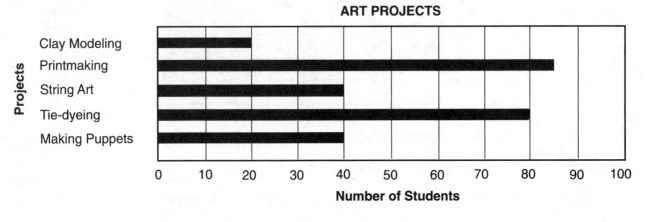

1. Is this a vertical bar graph or a horizontal bar graph? _____

2. What do the numbers below the graph show? _____

3. What does each interval of the scale represent? _____

4. Which project was most popular? _____

5. Which project was least popular? _____

Mixed Applications

Use the graph above to answer Exercises 6–7.

6. How many students chose
printmaking or tie-dyeing?

_____

7. How many students chose an
art project?

_____

MIXED REVIEW

Write the three other facts for each family of facts.

1. 8 × 6 = 48

2. 56 ÷ 7 = 8

3. 6 × 7 = 42

_____   _____   _____

_____   _____   _____

_____   _____   _____

48

Exploring
Making a Bar Graph

Will and his friends earned money during the summer.

1. Use the table to make a
   bar graph. Remember:

   • Choose a scale.
   • Label the graph.
   • Write a title for the graph.

Lawns Mowed This Summer	
Name	**Number**
Will	6
Taylor	10
Joaquin	8
Barb	4
Steve	3

Mixed Applications

Use the graph you made to help you answer Exercises 2–3.

2. Who had mowed the greatest
   number of lawns?

   _____

3. How many lawns did Will and his
   friends mow in all?

   _____

WRITER'S CORNER

4. Take a survey of your friends'
   favorite summer activities. Make
   a bar graph to show the
   information. Explain what the
   bar graph shows.

   _____

   _____

Graphing Points on a Grid

Use the grid to answer Exercises 1–12.

Write the letter for each point.

1. (4,2) _____   2. (9,6) _____

3. (2,1) _____   4. (8,7) _____

5. (6,4) _____   6. (10,8) _____

Write the ordered pair for each letter.

7. A _____   8. V _____

9. N _____   10. E _____

11. F _____   12. I _____

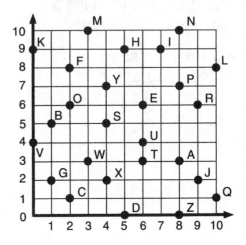

Mixed Applications

Use the grid for Exercises 13–14.

13. Which letters on the grid have a 5 in the ordered pair that gives their location? Write the letters and the ordered pairs on the line below.

_____

14. Think of a word. Have a family member use ordered pairs to spell out your word.

LANGUAGE ARTS CONNECTION

Use the letters at the points to solve the riddle. Move right and up to find each letter.

15. What does a leopard say when it rains?
(5,9) (4,7) (6,6) (5,9)   (4,7) (7,8) (5,9) (7,3)
(5,9) (4,7) (8,10)   (7,3) (9,1) (5,0) (5,9)

_____

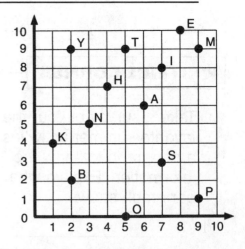

Line Graphs

Use the graph to answer Exercises 1–5.

The sporting goods store made a line graph to show the number of sales for six months.

1. During which month was the number of sales greatest? _____

2. During which month was the number of sales least? _____

3. How many sales were there in

   September? _____ November? _____ July? _____

Mixed Applications

Use the graph above to answer Exercises 4–7.

4. In which two months were the number of sales the same?

   _____

5. In which two months were the number of sales less than 150?

   _____

6. Between which two months did the number of sales decrease?

   _____

7. Find the total number of sales for the six-month period.

   _____

VISUAL THINKING

Think about how the first two figures are related.
Choose the correct answer.

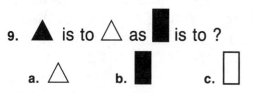

8. ◯ is to ◯ as ▢ is to ?

   a. ◯   b. ▢   c. ◇

9. ▲ is to △ as ▮ is to ?

   a. △   b. ▮   c. ▯

Exploring
Making a Line Graph

Michele looked up the average temperatures for October through March in Miami, Florida. Her findings are in this table.

1. Complete the line graph to show how the temperature changed. Use the table to help you.

Month	Average Temperature
October	78°F
November	72°F
December	68°F
January	67°F
February	68°F
March	71°F

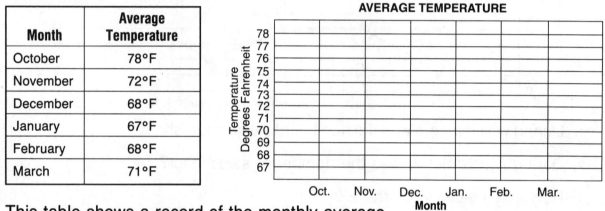

2. This table shows a record of the monthly average rainfall in days for Miami, Florida. Use the data to make a line graph.

Month	Jan.	Feb.	Mar.	Apr.	May	June	July	Aug.	Sept.	Oct.	Nov.	Dec.
Days of Rain	6	5	6	7	10	13	16	16	18	15	8	7

LOGICAL REASONING

3. A blue box has 5 times as many marbles as a red box. The blue box has 24 more marbles than the red box. How many marbles are in each box?

Problem Solving
Analyze Data to Make Decisions

Make a different type of graph for each situation.

1. The Villa family traveled by car from New Mexico to California. In one afternoon Ramón counted buses, vans, tractors, and trucks. Create the data and graph the number of vehicles.

2. The Villa family spent $40 on food the first day. They spent $5 more the next day. Create the rest of the data. Draw a graph. Show how the amount spent on food changed over 7 days.

| Mixed Applications > STRATEGIES | • Find a Pattern • Use a Table • Analyze Data to Make Decisions • Use a Graph |

Use the graph to answer Exercises 3–5.

3. In which states did the Villas travel over 300 miles?

_____

4. How many more miles did they travel in New Mexico than in California?

_____

5. How many miles did they travel in all?

_____

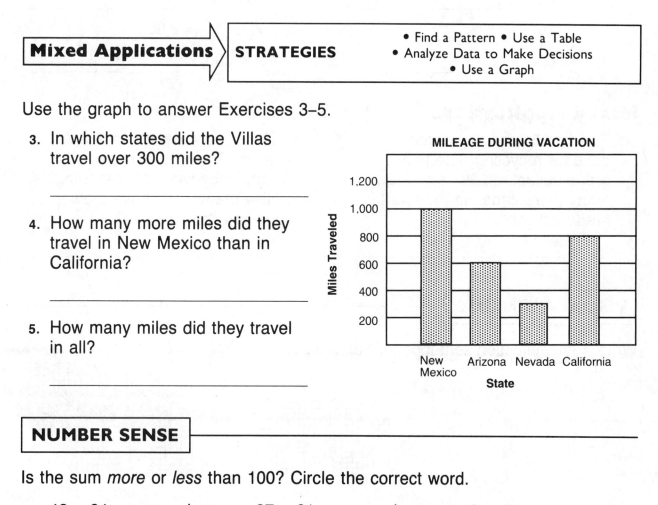

MILEAGE DURING VACATION

Miles Traveled

1,200
1,000
800
600
400
200

New Mexico   Arizona   Nevada   California

State

NUMBER SENSE

Is the sum *more* or *less* than 100? Circle the correct word.

6. 42 + 64   more   less   7. 27 + 81   more   less   8. 19 + 79   more   less

Exploring Patterns and Mental Math

1. Write the product on the place-value chart.

    2 × 3 = 2 × 3 ones ⟶

    2 × 30 = 2 × 3 tens ⟶

    2 × 300 = 2 × 3 hundreds ⟶

    2 × 3,000 = 2 × 3 thousands ⟶

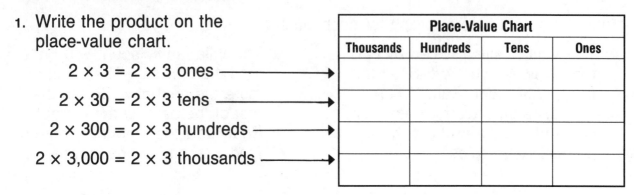

Place-Value Chart			
Thousands	Hundreds	Tens	Ones

Complete each pattern.

2.   3 × 4 = _____

   3 × 40 = _____

   3 × 400 = _____

   3 × 4,000 = _____

3.   7 × _____ = 28

   7 × 40 = _____

   7 × _____ = 2,800

   7 × 4,000 = _____

Mixed Applications

4. The fourth grade collected 347 cans for recycling. The fifth grade collected 289 cans. How many more cans did the fourth grade collect?

   _____

5. There are 4 people in Joan's family. Each person saves 5 cans each week for recycling. How many cans have they saved after 3 weeks?

   _____

VISUAL THINKING ──────────────────

Write a multiplication sentence for each picture.

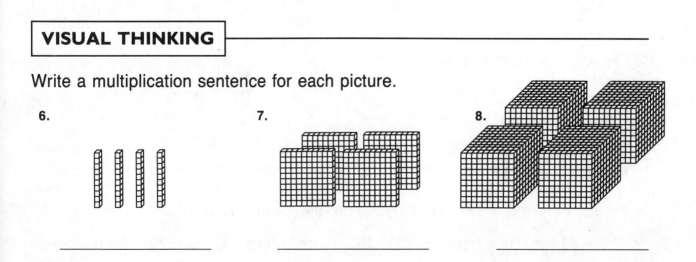

6.

_____

7.

_____

8.

_____

Estimating Products

Estimate the product by using front-end digits.

1. 4 × 42 _____   2. 3 × 348 _____   3. 6 × 2,240 _____

Estimate the product by rounding.

4. 9 × 43 _____   5. 3 × 347 _____   6. 4 × 5,729 _____

Estimate the product.

7. 52	8. 69	9. 472	10. 4,016	11. 607
× 3	× 6	× 7	× 7	× 5

Mixed Applications

12. Karin rides 38 kilometers to and from work each day. About how many kilometers is this in a five-day work week?

_____

13. At Karin's workplace, there are 18 workers in each office. If there are 8 offices, about how many workers are there?

_____

14. In one month, Karin spends about $50 on gas for her car, $22 for parking, and $48 on bus tickets. About how much money does Karin spend on transportation in a month?

_____

15. Karin begins work at 8:15 A.M. She eats her lunch from 12:15 P.M. until 12:45 P.M. and then goes back to work. She quits working for the day at 4:30 P.M. How many hours a day does Karin work?

_____

LOGICAL REASONING

Underline the problem with the greater product.

16. 3 × 67	17. 30 × 9	18. 7 × 84	19. 83 × 5
67 × 4	6 × 40	84 × 8	6 × 72

Exploring Multiplication

Find each product using place-value blocks on a mat
and the partial product method.

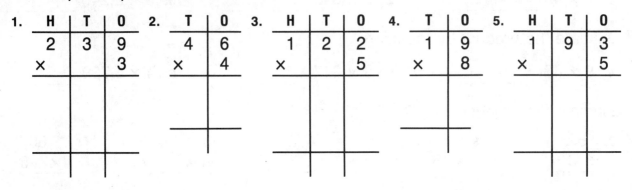

1.
H	T	O
2	3	9
×		3

2.
T	O
4	6
×	4

3.
H	T	O
1	2	2
×		5

4.
T	O
1	9
×	8

5.
H	T	O
1	9	3
×		5

Mixed Applications

6. Julia's family pays $18 a day to
rent skis. How much will they
pay for 4 days of ski rentals?

_____

7. A ticket for the ski lift costs $22
per person for one day. How
much will 3 people pay for lift
tickets for 4 days?

_____

EVERYDAY MATH CONNECTION

8. Complete the table to show the different ways you
can have $24 using the bills shown.

Ten-Dollar Bill	Five-Dollar Bill	One-Dollar Bill

Multiplying Two-Digit Numbers

Find the product.

1. 62
    × 4

2. 67
    × 3

3. 41
    × 6

4. 78
    × 3

5. 93
    × 9

6. 9 × 46 _____

7. 2 × 47 _____

8. 5 × 36 _____

Mixed Applications

9. The scout troop sold calendars to raise money. There are 28 children in the troop. Each child sold 5 calendars. How many calendars did the troop sell?

_____

10. There are 6 scout troops going on an overnight camping trip. Each troop is sending 17 children. How many children are going on the trip?

_____

11. Jason bought a new sleeping bag. It usually sells for $89.95, but it was on sale for $72.50. How much money did Jason save by buying it on sale?

_____

12. The scouts will leave for their trip at 6:30 A.M. They will travel for 3 hours and 15 minutes. What time will it be when they arrive at the campsite?

_____

HEALTH CONNECTION

A **calorie** is a measure of the energy produced by food. This table lists some of the foods the scouts will have on their trip. Use the table to find the total number of calories in each of these meals.

Food	Calories
Milk (1 glass)	100
Apple	70
Bread (1 slice)	65
Cheese (1 slice)	84
Carrot Strip	20
Raisins (1 small box)	185
Soup (1 cup)	98

13. 2 glasses of milk
    1 apple
    2 cups of soup

_____

14. 2 slices of bread
    3 slices of cheese
    1 box of raisins

_____

15. 8 carrot strips
    1 glass of milk
    4 slices of cheese

_____

Multiplying Three-Digit Numbers

Find the product.

1. 287
    × 2

2. 114
    × 3

3. 317
    × 3

4. 175
    × 5

5. 248
    × 3

6. 182
    × 4

7. 385
    × 2

8. 319
    × 3

9. 136
    × 5

10. 246
    × 4

11. 2 × 406 _____

12. 3 × 275 _____

13. 5 × 176 _____

14. 3 × 318 _____

15. 4 × 193 _____

16. 4 × 217 _____

Mixed Applications

17. An office building has 135 offices on each floor. How many offices are on 5 floors?

    _____

18. There are 248 offices that need 2 lamps and 164 offices that need 1 lamp. How many offices in all need lamps?

    _____

NUMBER SENSE

Sometimes you can use mental math to multiply.

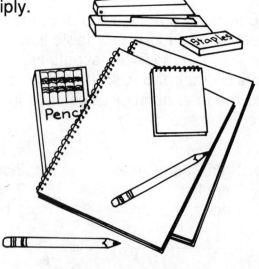

Multiply.   4 × 206 = ☐

Think:
    4 × 6 = 24
    4 × 200 = 800
    800 + 24 = 824

Use mental math to multiply.

19. 6 × 107 _____

20. 3 × 208 _____

21. 4 × 205 _____

Problem-Solving Strategy
Work Backward

Solve. Make a flowchart and work backward.

1. Elena bought a belt for $12 and a scarf for $6. Later, her mother gave her $10. Then Elena had $15. How much money did she have before she bought the belt and scarf?

   _____

2. Dan and Julie played a number game. First, Dan picked a number and added 8. Then, he multiplied by 4. Last, he subtracted 5. The result was 35. What number did Dan pick?

   _____

Mixed Applications > **STRATEGIES** • Write a Number Sentence • Work Backward • Draw a Picture

Choose a strategy and solve.

3. Peter rides his bike 3 kilometers each day. How many kilometers does he ride in 30 days?

   _____

4. Eric is 2 inches shorter than Peter and 3 inches taller than Julie. Jill is 2 inches shorter than Julie. Who is the tallest?

   _____

5. Dan rode his bike after he ate dinner. He watched television before dinner. He did his homework after he rode his bike. What was the second thing Dan did?

   _____

MIXED REVIEW

Write the time in two different ways.

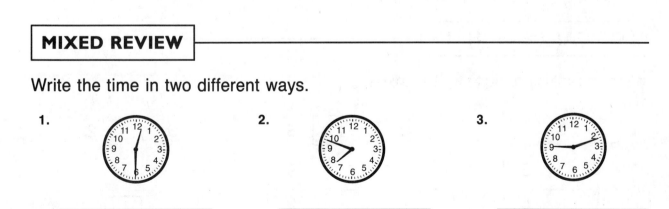

1. _____ _____

2. _____ _____

3. _____ _____

Multiplying

More Practice

Find the product.

1. 328
   × 6

2. 473
   × 4

3. 279
   × 7

4. 305
   × 3

5. 725
   × 5

6. 458
   × 8

7. 483
   × 5

8. 286
   × 3

9. 940
   × 9

10. 495
    × 6

11. 3 × 534 _____

12. 8 × 206 _____

13. 7 × 992 _____

Mixed Applications

14. The fair opens at 8:00 A.M. It closes at 11:00 P.M. How many hours each day is the fair open?

    _____

15. An adult ticket to the fair costs $4. A child's ticket cost $2. The Alders pay for 2 adult tickets and 3 child's tickets. How much do they pay?

    _____

16. There are 156 booths at the fair. Three people work at each booth. How many people work at the booths?

    _____

17. There are 527 seats in the arena. Shows are given 4 days each week. All the seats are filled. How many people see the show each week?

    _____

LOGICAL REASONING

Write the missing digits in the boxes.

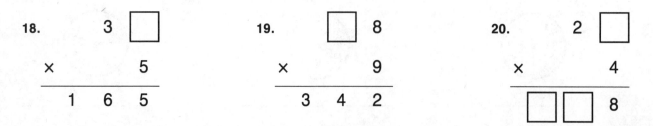

18.   3 ☐
     ×   5
     ─────────
       1 6 5

19.   ☐ 8
     ×   9
     ─────────
       3 4 2

20.   2 ☐
     ×   4
     ─────────
     ☐ ☐ 8

60

Multiplying Larger Numbers

Estimate. Then use a calculator to find the product.

1. $\begin{array}{r} 2,096 \\ \times \quad 2 \\ \hline \end{array}$ 2. $\begin{array}{r} 1,786 \\ \times \quad 4 \\ \hline \end{array}$ 3. $\begin{array}{r} 4,365 \\ \times \quad 3 \\ \hline \end{array}$ 4. $\begin{array}{r} 7,258 \\ \times \quad 4 \\ \hline \end{array}$ 5. $\begin{array}{r} 6,518 \\ \times \quad 7 \\ \hline \end{array}$

6. $7 \times 3,624 =$ _____   7. $6 \times 4,633 =$ _____

8. $3 \times 7,214 =$ _____   9. $8 \times 2,715 =$ _____

Mixed Applications

10. The *Morning News* prints 4,750 copies of the newspaper each day. How many copies are printed in 5 days?

_____

11. Each delivery truck can be loaded with 1,086 newspapers. How many newspapers can be loaded onto 3 trucks?

_____

12. Shana delivers the Sunday papers. She starts her route at 6:15 A.M. and finishes at 7:50 A.M. How long does it take Shana to deliver the Sunday papers?

_____

13. Isaac has 125 customers for Sunday newspaper delivery and 84 customers for weekday delivery. Of the customers who get Sunday delivery, 32 also get weekday delivery. How many customers does Isaac have in all?

_____

WRITER'S CORNER

14. Suppose you are trying to get new customers for your paper route. Write what you would tell people in order to get them to sign up.

_____

_____

_____

Problem Solving
Choose the Method of Computation

This table lists different methods of computation. It tells how to decide on the best method to use to solve the problem. Tell which method of computation you would use to solve the problem. Solve.

Method	Example
Calculator	Use with large numbers or when you need an answer quickly.
Mental Math	Use with small numbers and multiples of tens, hundreds, thousands, and so on.
Objects	Use objects to model the situation.
Paper and Pencil	Use when a calculator is not available and the problem is too difficult to solve mentally.

1. A kennel uses 86 packs of dog food in one month. There are 6 cans in each pack. How many cans is this each month?

2. The kennel has 10 outdoor dog runs. Six dogs can be placed in each run. How many dogs can be outdoors at once?

Mixed Applications > STRATEGIES
• Draw a Picture
• Work Backward • Write a Number Sentence

3. Kris lives between Hope's house and Central Park. Hope lives between Kris and Sharon. Martha lives closer to the park than Kris. Who lives farthest from the park?

4. Jim bought a sweater for $18 and a tie for $9. Later, his father gave him $10. Then Jim had $13. How much money did Jim have before he bought the sweater and the tie?

VISUAL THINKING

Tell how many blocks are in the pile.

5.

Think: 4 in a row, 3 rows, 2 layers

$(4 \times 3) \times 2 =$ _____ blocks

6.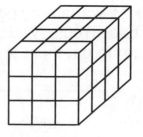

Multiplying Using Money

Estimate by rounding to the next higher dime, dollar, or ten dollars. Then find the product.

1. $6.38 $\longrightarrow$ $7.00
   × 3 $\longrightarrow$ × 3

2. $0.72 $\longrightarrow$
   × 9 $\longrightarrow$

3. $4.52 $\longrightarrow$
   × 6 $\longrightarrow$

4. $42.85 $\longrightarrow$
   × 3 $\longrightarrow$

5. $15.76 $\longrightarrow$
   × 4 $\longrightarrow$

6. $5.29 $\longrightarrow$
   × 4 $\longrightarrow$

7. $0.82 $\longrightarrow$
   × 5 $\longrightarrow$

8. $46.71 $\longrightarrow$
   × 6 $\longrightarrow$

9. $9.82 $\longrightarrow$
   × 8 $\longrightarrow$

Find the product.

10. 9 × $2.94 _____

11. 3 × $0.47 _____

12. 8 × $1.45 _____

Mixed Applications

13. The school orchestra bought 3 sets of cymbals. Each set cost $32.85. How much did the orchestra spend in all?

14. The orchestra bought 6 new music stands. Each music stand cost $9.84. Estimate the cost of the music stands to the nearest dollar.

CONSUMER CONNECTION

Find the cost of each shopping list.

15. 3 cassette tapes
    1 album

16. 4 videos
    1 CD

17. 3 albums
    5 videos

18. 4 CD's
    3 videos

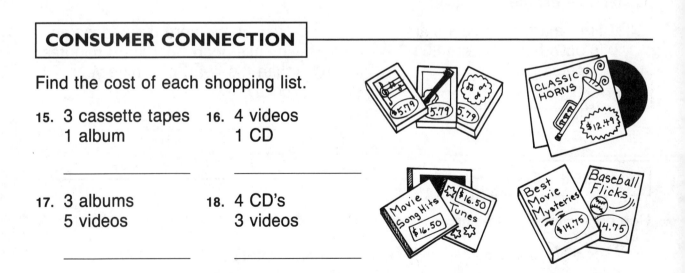

Multiplication
Using Mental Math

Use a basic fact and mental math to help you find
the product.

1. $10 \times 8 = $ _____

   $100 \times 8 = $ _____

   $100 \times 80 = $ _____

2. $7 \times 60 = $ _____

   $70 \times 60 = $ _____

   $700 \times 60 = $ _____

3. $60 \times 9 = $ _____

   $600 \times 9 = $ _____

   $600 \times 90 = $ _____

Find the product.

4. $\begin{array}{r} 60 \\ \times 10 \\ \hline \end{array}$

5. $\begin{array}{r} 2,000 \\ \times 400 \\ \hline \end{array}$

6. $\begin{array}{r} 8,000 \\ \times 70 \\ \hline \end{array}$

7. $\begin{array}{r} 600 \\ \times 800 \\ \hline \end{array}$

8. $\begin{array}{r} 30,000 \\ \times 600 \\ \hline \end{array}$

Mixed Applications

9. A person's heart beats about 70 times a minute. About how many times does the heart beat in 60 minutes?

   _____

10. A dog's heart beats about 100 times a minute. About how many times does a dog's heart beat in 20 minutes?

    _____

11. An infant's heart beats about 120 times a minute. The heart of a nine-year-old child beats about 90 times a minute.

    a. How many times does an infant's heart beat in 60 minutes?

    _____

    b. How many more times does an infant's heart beat in 60 minutes than the heart of a nine-year-old child?

    _____

NUMBER SENSE ─────────────────────────────

Compare. Write $<$, $>$, or $=$.

12. $40 \times 60 \bigcirc 4 \times 600$

13. $30 \times 80 \bigcirc 3 \times 8,000$

14. $70 \times 80 \bigcirc 7 \times 80$

15. $60 \times 70 \bigcirc 6 \times 700$

Estimating Products

Estimate the product by using front-end digits.

1. 13 × 64 _____
2. 48 × 29 _____
3. 63 × 87 _____

Estimate the product by rounding.

4. 14 × 57 _____
5. 39 × 25 _____
6. 61 × 88 _____

Round to the nearest dollar. Estimate the product.

7. 17 × $4.79 _____
8. 58 × $9.09 _____
9. 45 × $1.14 _____

Round to the nearest ten cents. Estimate the product.

10. 22 × $3.39 _____
11. 68 × $2.15 _____
12. 71 × $1.09 _____

Mixed Applications

13. A mail carrier delivers mail on 18 streets each day. Each street has 56 houses. About how many houses are on the mail carrier's route?

14. The post office sells booklets of stamps with 20 stamps in each booklet. Each stamp costs $0.29. About how much does each booklet cost?

LOGICAL REASONING

Mental math can help you multiply.

Example   50 × 24 = ☐?☐

Think: 100 is twice as much as 50. So 100 times a number is twice as much as 50 times a number.
100 × 24 = 2,400
So,   50 × 24 = 1,200

15.   100 × 64 = 6,400

So,   50 × 64 = _____

16.   100 × 25 = 2,500

So,   50 × 25 = _____

17.   100 × 88 = 8,800

So,   50 × 88 = _____

18.   100 × 66 = 6,600

So,   50 × 66 = _____

Multiplication
Multiples of 10

Complete. Find the value of *n*.

1. 50   × 18 = *n*

    10 × _____ × 18 = *n*

    10 × _____ = _____

2. 35   ×   40   = *n*

    35   × 4 × _____ = *n*

    _____ × 10   = _____

Find the product.

3. 52
    × 30

4. 23
    × 50

5. 15
    × 20

6. 32
    × 30

7. 41
    × 60

8. 36
    × 40

9. 40 × 54 = _____

10. 50 × 78 = _____

11. 80 × 67 = _____

Mixed Applications

Use the table to help you answer Exercises 12–16.

| 60 minutes = 1 hour |
| 24 hours = 1 day |

How many minutes are there in

12. 12 hours? _____

13. 1 day? _____

How many hours are there in

14. 1 week? _____

15. 10 days? _____

16. Suppose you sleep 8 hours each night.
    How many minutes are you awake each day? _____

WRITER'S CORNER

17. Use this data to write two multiplication questions.

| 60 seconds = 1 minute |
| 60 minutes = 1 hour |

_____

_____

Problem-Solving Strategy
Make a Graph

The class took a survey to find out the different ways the students in their grade got to school. They made a table of the data.

Transportation to School	
Type	**Number of Students**
Bus	18
Car	5
Walking	7
Bicycle	10

1. Make a bar graph using the information from the table. Remember to:

   • decide whether you want a vertical or horizontal graph.
   • choose a scale.
   • label the graph.
   • write a title for the graph.

Mixed Applications

STRATEGIES	• Find a Pattern • Choose the Operation • Work Backward • Make a Table • Write a Number Sentence

Choose a strategy and solve.

2. Clara bought 2 books. Each book cost $6. Then she spent $10 for a CD. How much money did Clara start with if she had $4 left?

   _____

3. The PTA is raising money for a bicycle rack that costs $225. They raise $8 the first week, then double the amount raised each week. How long will it take them to raise enough money?

   _____

WRITER'S CORNER

4. Survey your friends to find out how they get to school. Make a bar graph for this information. Write three sentences that explain your graph.

   _____

   _____

Exploring Two-Digit Factors

Solve using partial products. Then solve using the shorter way.

1. 29   29
   ×66   ×66

2. 87   87
   ×16   ×16

3. 91   91
   ×46   ×46

Mixed Applications

Write a number sentence. Solve.

4. Liu delivers 14 papers on Wood Street. Each paper has 24 pages. How many pages are in all 14 papers?

_____

5. Mr. DeLano ordered newspapers for his class. He ordered 26 papers each day for 19 days. How many newspapers were ordered in all?

_____

MIXED REVIEW

Find the product.

1. 5 × 60 = _____

2. 8 × 500 = _____

3. 4 × 8,000 = _____

4. 7 × 400 = _____

5. 9 × 3,000 = _____

6. 8 × 900 = _____

Complete. Find the value of n.

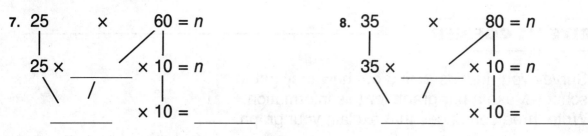

7. 25   ×   60 = n
   | / |
   25 × _____ / × 10 = n
     \   / |
      \   /   × 10 =
   _____   _____

8. 35   ×   80 = n
   | / |
   35 × _____ / × 10 = n
     \   / |
      \   /   × 10 =
   _____   _____

68

Multiplying by Two-Digit Numbers

Find the product.

1. 57 ×32	2. 36 ×96	3. 84 ×17	4. 62 ×45	5. 79 ×24

6. 76 ×48	7. 39 ×23	8. 90 ×75	9. 29 ×63	10. 56 ×42

11. $40 \times 78 = n$ _____   12. $42 \times 57 = n$ _____

13. $26 \times 43 = n$ _____   14. $68 \times 46 = n$ _____

Mixed Applications

15. A car dealer works 42 hours each week. How many hours does the car dealer work in one year (52 weeks)?

16. Tina drives 18 miles to work. She drives home using the same route. How far does Tina drive in a 21-day work month?

CONSUMER CONNECTION

The fuel economy of a car tells how many miles it can travel on one gallon of gasoline.

How many miles can each car travel on a full tank of gasoline?

17. Sunburst _____   18. RX-10 _____

19. TZK-2 _____   20. Delray _____

Model of Car	Fuel Economy	Number of Gallons in Tank
Sunburst	32	12
RX-10	36	18
TZK-2	30	24
Delray	28	22

Multiplying
More Practice

Find the product.

1. 345
  × 12

2. 342
  × 68

3. 164
  × 53

4. 304
  × 82

5. 657
  × 89

6. 89 × 508 _____

7. 62 × 258 _____

8. 56 × 613 _____

Mixed Applications

9. There are 123 dancers in the ballet. Each dancer has 12 costumes. How many costumes are there?

10. In one ballet, there are 14 adult male dancers, 14 adult female dancers, and 10 young dancers. How many dancers is that?

EVERYDAY MATH CONNECTION

Al is looking for a part-time job. The table lists the jobs and the weekly salary for which he applied.

11. Complete the Yearly Salary column in the table. Remember, there are 52 weeks in a year.

12. Which job pays the highest salary?

Part-time Jobs

Job	Weekly Salary	Yearly Salary
Typist	$85	
Dishwasher	$90	
Cashier	$115	
Stock clerk	$72	
Delivery person	$120	

13. How much more money would Al earn for the year as a delivery person than as a dishwasher?

14. If you were Al, what questions would you ask before you decided which job you wanted?

Using Multiplication

First estimate. Then find the product.

1. 108
    × 87

2. 463
    × 34

3. 2,786
    × 43

4. 8,157
    × 92

5. 20,016
    × 45

6. 40 × 768 _____

7. 24 × 5,063 _____

8. 36 × 895 _____

9. 74 × 10,572 _____

Barbara placed an order with a wholesale bulb
company for her garden center. Complete the table.

Bulb Order

	Type of Bulb	Number of Cartons	Bulbs in Each Carton	Total Number of Bulbs
10.	Crocuses	42	250	
11.	Tulips	865	75	
12.	Daffodils	460	50	

Mixed Applications

13. Barbara plants 15 tulip bulbs in
    each of 150 clay pots. How many
    bulbs does she use?

    _____

14. Mrs. Daley buys 8 amaryllis
    bulbs. Each bulb costs $8.79.
    How much change should Mrs.
    Daley receive if she gives the
    clerk $80.00?

    _____

MIXED REVIEW

Find the product.

1. $0.84
    × 6

2. $1.56
    × 9

3. $3.09
    × 4

4. 156
    × 97

5. 825
    × 88

Problem-Solving Strategy
Guess and Check

Guess the answer. Then check it.

1. There are 25 plants in Tamara's garden. There are 4 times as many tomato plants as bean plants. How many tomato and bean plants are planted?

   _____

   _____

2. José worked on a jigsaw puzzle for 6 hours. He worked 2 more hours in the afternoon than after dinner. How long did he work in the afternoon and after dinner?

   _____

   _____

Mixed Applications ⟩ STRATEGIES	• Make a Table • Draw a Picture • Find a Pattern • Work Backward • Write a Number Sentence • Make a Graph

3. Four girls are racing. Gail is behind Hilda. Ingrid is ahead of Hilda. Jill is ahead of Gail, but behind Hilda. Which girl is in second place?

   _____

4. Seth knits striped blankets. The first stripe is blue, the second is yellow, and the third is green. This pattern repeats. What color is the ninth stripe?

   _____

5. Les bought a set of 3 shells for $25.00 and a frame to display the shells for $18.95. How much money did he pay for these items?

   _____

6. Jerry bought a $15 game and a $6 book. Later, Dad gave him $20. Then Jerry had $31. How much money did Jerry have before he bought the game and book?

   _____

NUMBER SENSE

Find the missing factor.

7. $80 \times$ _____ $= 5,600$

8. $9 \times$ _____ $= 72,000$

9. $600 \times$ _____ $= 6,000$

10. $6 \times$ _____ $= 42,000$

11. $500 \times$ _____ $= 10,000$

12. $40 \times$ _____ $= 32,000$

13. $100 \times$ _____ $= 7,500$

14. $30 \times$ _____ $= 9,000$

15. $7 \times$ _____ $= 49,000$

Multiplying Using Money

Find the product. You may use a calculator.

1.	$4.29 × 52	2.	$2.46 × 46	3.	$24.78 × 74	4.	$0.68 × 23	5.	$23.75 × 63

6.	$7.89 × 42	7.	$5.09 × 24	8.	$0.63 × 85	9.	$13.79 × 39	10.	$45.06 × 78

11. 10 × $8.34 _____ 12. 82 × $4.35 _____ 13. 46 × $51.89 _____

Mixed Applications

Use the table to solve Exercises 14–16.

14. A total of 39 children came by bus to the ski lodge. Each child bought a lift ticket. How much money did they spend?

_____

Downhill Ski Slope Fees

	Adult	Child
Ski Rental	$18.75	$ 9.50
Boot Rental	$ 7.50	$ 3.75
Lift Tickets	$18.00	$12.00
Lesson (30 minute)	$21.75	$12.50

15. The ski lodge rented 43 pairs of adult skis on Thursday. How much money did the lodge collect?

_____

16. Mr. and Mrs. Rentas and their 3 children rented boots and skis and bought lift tickets. Two of the children took a 30-minute lesson. How much money

    did the Rentas family spend? _____

LOGICAL REASONING

You may write *pennies, nickels, dimes, quarters,* and *half-dollars* to answer Exercises 17 and 18.

17. What 6 coins make $0.47?

18. What 50 coins make $1.00?

_____   _____

_____   _____

Exploring Units of Measure

Find the length of each object in centimeters and in inches.
Use rulers and string. Record your measurements.

	Object	Centimeters	Inches
1.	a marker		
2.	a crayon		
3.	a paper clip		
4.	height of your chair		
5.	a folder		
6.	a pencil		
7.	a calculator		

Solve.

8. Lee wants to make a picture frame with wood. She needs 96 inches of framing. Lee has two 45-inch strips of wood. Does she have enough wood for the frame? Explain your answer.

_____

_____

9. If you measure the length of a book in centimeters, inches, and a unit you invent, which measurement will have the fewest units?

_____

_____

WRITER'S CORNER

10. Do you think it would be easier to estimate the length of an object using nonstandard units, inches, or centimeters? Explain your answer.

_____

_____

_____

_____

Length
Metric Units

Ring the more reasonable answer.

1.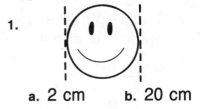

   a. 2 cm   b. 20 cm

2.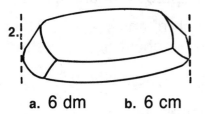

   a. 6 dm   b. 6 cm

3.

   a. 1 dm   b. 10 dm

Choose the appropriate unit for each. Write *cm, dm, m,* or *km.*

4. height of your desk _____

5. length of a school hallway _____

6. length of a river _____

7. length of a stapler _____

Ring the longer unit.

8. 5 cm or 5 dm   9. 10 m or 10 dm   10. 16 km or 16 dm   11. 2 m or 2 cm

Mixed Applications

12. Jenny runs 7 km a day for 1 week. How many km does she run in that period of time?

    _____

13. Enrique has twice as many stickers as Bob. Fay has 8 more stickers than Bob. Roy has 5 fewer stickers than Fay. Roy has 10 stickers. Who has the most stickers?

    _____

VISUAL THINKING

14. What is the distance in km from
    a. Pink to Penk? _____
    b. Penk to Pank? _____
    c. Pink to Pank? _____

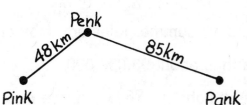

Length
Customary Units

Choose the appropriate unit for each. Write *in., ft, yd,* or *mi.*

1. The length of an envelope is about

   9 _____

2. The height of a street lamp is about

   9 _____

3. The length of a hallway is about

   3 _____

Ring the longer unit.

4. 3 ft or 3 yd

5. 16 ft or 16 in.

6. 23 mi or 23 yd

7. 400 in. or 400 yd

Mixed Applications

8. Marvin is 5 feet tall. His brother Mel is 2 yards tall. Who is taller?

   _____

9. Would it be more appropriate to use a ruler or a yardstick to measure the width of a desk?

   _____

Use the table for Exercises 10–12.

10. Which river is longer than 2,000 miles?

    _____

11. How long is Snake River?

    _____

Lengths of U.S. Rivers	
River	Length in Miles
Ohio	1,310
Copper	286
Snake	1,040
Mississippi	2,340
Tennessee	886

Source: 1990 Almanac

12. Name the river whose length is about three times greater than the length of Copper River.

    _____

SCIENCE CONNECTION

Complete each sentence with the appropriate unit of measure. Write *in., ft, yd,* or *mi.*

13. A heavy summer rainstorm may bring about 2 _____ of rain.

14. Earth is about 93,000,000 _____ from the sun.

15. The height of a redwood tree may be more than 300 _____ .

Problem-Solving Strategy
Draw a Picture

Draw a picture to solve.

1. At the zoo, Ruth fed the monkeys before she fed the bears and after she fed the ducks. She fed the elephants last. What animals did she feed first?

   _____

2. Ralph lives the farthest from school. Diane lives between Cheryl and Ralph. Gina lives closer to school than Cheryl. Who lives between Gina and Diane?

   _____

3. Hope arranged her chips in a row. Every third chip is red. The first and last chips are green. All of the other chips are blue. There are 10 chips. How are the chips arranged?

   _____

   _____

4. Francisca is shorter than Alex and taller than Stacy. Stacy is taller than Kitty. Who is the tallest?

   _____

Mixed Applications ⟩ **STRATEGIES** • Write a Number Sentence • Guess and Check • Work Backward • Make a Graph

Choose a strategy and solve.

5. Michael paid a sale price of $42.99 for a jacket. The regular price of the jacket was $50.00. How much did Michael save?

   _____

6. Maya grew 1 dm taller this year. Her brother, Gordon, grew 12 cm taller. Who grew more? How much more?

   _____

WRITER'S CORNER

7. Write a problem that can be solved using the *Draw a Picture* strategy.

   _____

Exploring
Measuring Perimeter

Use an inch ruler and a string to find the perimeter of each.

1. your chair seat _____

2. a library book _____

3. a calculator _____

4. a folder _____

Write a number sentence to find the perimeter of each figure. Solve.

5.

3 cm   3 cm

2 cm   2 cm

5 cm

_____

_____

6.

4 cm

4 cm   4 cm

4 cm   4 cm

4 cm   4 cm

4 cm

_____

_____

Solve. You may use a calculator.

7. A rectangle is 6 in. long and 12 in. wide. Find the perimeter.

_____

8. A square measures 13 cm on each side. Find the perimeter.

_____

MIXED REVIEW

Find the product.

1. 1,197
    ×   6

2.   56
    × 40

3.   32
    × 24

4.   71
    × 62

5.   372
    × 21

Tell how much time has elapsed.

6.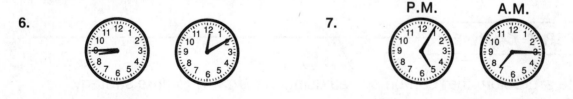

7.
P.M.   A.M.

_____   _____

78

Exploring Customary Units of Capacity

Choose the appropriate unit of measure.
Write *t, tbsp, c, pt, qt,* or *gal.*

1.

_____

2.

_____

3.
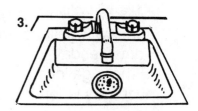

_____

4.

_____

5.
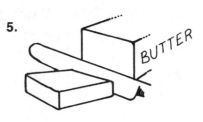

_____

6.

_____

Solve.

7. José pours 1 cup of apple juice and 3 cups of grape juice into a large bottle. How many pints of juice are in the bottle?

_____

8. Louise brings a 3-gallon jug of water to share at the tennis game. If each person drinks 1 quart of water, how many persons can drink from this jug?

_____

EVERYDAY MATH CONNECTION

When Wanda copied the recipes below, she left out the units of liquid capacity. Use logical reasoning to help you determine a sensible unit for each blank.

9. Fruit Punch—32 servings

2 _____ of grape juice

1 _____ of apple juice

1 _____ of lemon juice

10. Tomato Noodle Soup—10 servings

2 _____ of beef broth

1 _____ of tomato juice

3 _____ of cooked noodles

Problem Solving
Multistep Problems

Use more than one step to solve.

1. The gas tank in the school bus holds 32 gallons of gas. On Monday, 8 gallons are used. From Tuesday to Wednesday, 16 more gallons are used. How much gas is left in the bus?

   _____

2. Martha left school at 3:15. She spent 15 minutes on safety patrol duty. It took 20 minutes to get home. How many minutes does Martha have left to rest before her tap class at 4:30?

   _____

3. The Ronald family is driving 1,353 miles from Memphis to Boston. They drive 324 miles on the first day and 372 miles the second day. How many miles are left?

   _____

4. Miami gets about 5 feet of rain each year. Atlanta gets about 4 feet each year. How many inches of rain falls in a year in both cities combined?

   _____

Mixed Applications	STRATEGIES	• Draw a Picture • Guess and Check • Work Backward

Choose a strategy and solve.

5. Ray spent $3 on a magazine. He spent half of his remaining money on a poster. Then, he spent $2 on a snack. Ray had $12 left after that. How much did Ray have to begin with?

   _____

6. A sparkle flashlight costs 15¢ more than a plain flashlight. The total cost for both flashlights is 99¢. What is the cost of each flashlight?

   _____

   _____

WRITER'S CORNER

7. Write a problem that requires more than one step to solve.

   _____

   _____

Capacity
Metric Units

Choose the appropriate unit of measure. Write *mL* or *L*.

1. a large milk bottle _____

2. a bowl of soup _____

3. water in a pool _____

4. a small can of juice _____

Ring the correct measure.

5.

   1 mL or 1 L

6.

   500 mL or 500 L

7.

   120 mL or 120 L

Ring the most reasonable measurement.

8. A water cooler holds about _____. a. 4 mL   b. 40 mL   c. 4 L

9. A jar of honey holds about _____. a. 65 mL   b. 650 mL   c. 65 L

10. A milk carton holds about _____. a. 20 mL   b. 2 L   c. 20 L

Mixed Applications

11. A tall vase holds about 2 L of water. A wide vase holds about 2,300 mL of water. Which holds more?

    _____

12. A large canteen provided each of 4 thirsty campers with 500 mL of water. How many liters of water did the canteen hold?

    _____

LOGICAL REASONING

Change each sentence so that it makes sense.

13. Jamie put 350 L of juice into her thermos.

    _____

14. Maureen put 200 mL of suntan lotion on before going in the sun.

    _____

15. Juana poured 2,500 mL of milk into her cereal.

    _____

16. Mr. Jacobs will paint his den with 4 mL of paint.

    _____

Mass
Metric Units

Choose the appropriate unit to weigh each item.
Write *g* or *kg.*

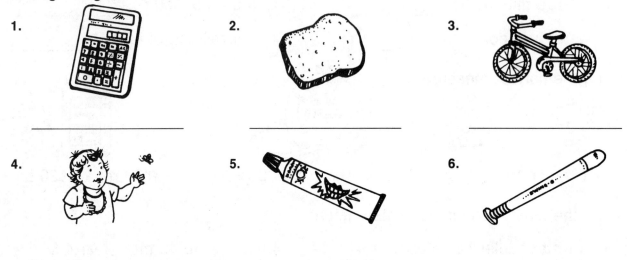

1. _____

2. _____

3. _____

4. _____

5. _____

6. _____

Ring the more reasonable measurement.

7. a feather   1 g or 100 g   8. a truck   175 kg or 1,750 kg

9. a pair of socks   20 g or 200 g   10. a piano   40 kg or 450 kg

Mixed Applications

11. Pete bought 4 loaves of bread. Each loaf weighs 750 grams. How many kilograms do all the loaves weigh?

    _____

12. Karen needs 1 kilogram of flour. She has 275 grams. How much more flour does Karen need?

    _____

LOGICAL REASONING _____

13. You need to fill a bag with 14 kg of oranges. How can you measure 14 kg of oranges using a balance scale and these weights: 1 kg, 5 kg, and 10 kg?

    _____

    _____

Weight
Customary Units

Choose the appropriate unit to measure. Write *oz, lb,* or *T.*

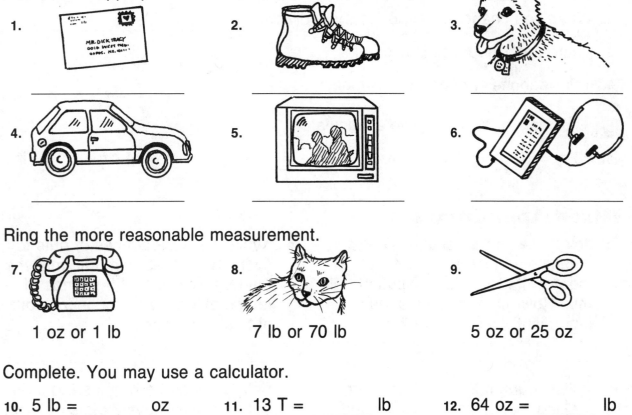

1. _____

2. _____

3. _____

4. _____

5. _____

6. _____

Ring the more reasonable measurement.

7. 1 oz or 1 lb

8. 7 lb or 70 lb

9. 5 oz or 25 oz

Complete. You may use a calculator.

10. 5 lb = _____ oz

11. 13 T = _____ lb

12. 64 oz = _____ lb

Mixed Applications

13. Harold says his large dog weighs 50. Does he mean pounds, ounces, or tons?

    _____

14. Mrs. Ming had six 12-ounce packages of rolls. What is the total weight? Use lb and oz.

    _____

EVERYDAY MATH CONNECTION

15. Rose's family recipe for stuffed mushrooms calls for 12 ounces of chopped meat to serve 4 people. How many pounds of chopped meat should Rose buy to serve 16 people?

    _____

Changing Units

Write *true* or *false* for each statement.

1. When you change feet to inches, you multiply. _____

2. When you change miles to feet, you divide. _____

3. There are 10 ounces in 1 pound. _____

4. Twelve inches are equal to 1 foot. _____

Complete. You may use a calculator.

5. 96 qt = _____ gal   6. 15 yd = _____ ft   7. 144 oz = _____ lb

Mixed Applications

8. Joy is making a trail mix. She combines equal parts of 4 ingredients to make a 2-pound trail mix. How many ounces of each ingredient does Joy use?

   _____

9. Kyoko added 2 ounces of nuts to every 10 ounces of muffin mix she made. If Kyoko had 5 pounds of muffin mix, how many ounces of nuts did she add?

   _____

10. Felicia bought 2 feet of gimp for making friendship bracelets. She uses an 8-inch strip of gimp to make each bracelet. How many bracelets can Felicia make?

    _____

11. Sally's punch bowl holds 6 quarts of liquid. She buys 2 pints of juice, 2 quarts of ginger ale, and 1 gallon of sherbet for a punch. Will all of the ingredients fit into the bowl?

    _____

NUMBER SENSE

Complete the tables. You may use a calculator.

12.

ft	1	2	3	4	5
in.					

13.

yd	3	6	9	12	15
ft					

14.

gal	1	2	3	4	5
pt					

15.

lb	2	4	6	8	10
oz					

Exploring Patterns in Division

Using what you have learned, tell how many digits there will be in each quotient.

1. 4)800
2. 3)9,000
3. 8)40
4. 6)1,800
5. 6)3,000

_____   _____   _____   _____   _____

Complete the pattern.

6. 6)24   6)240   6)2,400   7. 9)27   9)270   9)2,700

8. 5)40   5)400   5)4,000   9. 8)56   8)560   8)5,600

Find the quotient. Then continue each example by changing the dividend, using multiples of 10, 100, and 1,000 to make a pattern.

10. 4)28   11. 6)48   12. 5)45   13. 7)35

4)280   6)480   5)450   7)350

4)2,800   6)4,800   5)4,500   7)3,500

4)28,000   6)48,000   5)45,000   7)35,000

EVERYDAY MATH CONNECTION

14. The public library has 1,200 books to sell at a sale. An equal number of books are placed into 6 bookcases. How many books are in each bookcase? _____

15. The same number of books are placed on each shelf. If each of the 6 bookcases has 4 shelves, how many books are on each shelf? _____

Connecting Multiplication and Division

Complete.

1. $23 \div 3 = n$

Think:

$6 \times 3 = 18$

$7 \times 3 = 21$

$8 \times 3 = 24$

So, $23 \div 3 = n$.

$n =$ _____

2. $42 \div 5 = n$

Think:

$7 \times 5 =$ _____

$8 \times 5 =$ _____

$9 \times 5 =$ _____

So, $42 \div 5 = n$.

$n =$ _____

3. $35 \div 8 = n$

Think:

$3 \times 8 =$ _____

$4 \times 8 =$ _____

$5 \times 8 =$ _____

So, $35 \div 8 = n$.

$n =$ _____

Use multiplication to find the quotient.

4. $19 \div 4 =$ _____

5. $22 \div 3 =$ _____

6. $19 \div 3 =$ _____

7. $25 \div 7 =$ _____

Use this division example for Exercises 8–11.
Write the number for each part of the division problem named.

$$\overset{8 \ r6}{7\overline{)62}}$$

8. divisor _____

9. quotient _____

10. dividend _____

11. remainder _____

Mixed Applications

12. Cyclists lined up in rows of 5 bikes each for the race. How many rows are full if there are 28 cyclists? How many are in the unfilled row?

13. Each of Camp FunTime's buses can hold 38 passengers. How many passengers can 7 of the camp's buses hold?

LOGICAL REASONING

14. My quotient is 6, and my divisor is 7. My dividend is 45. I am the remainder. What number am I?

15. If you divide me by 8, my remainder is 7. I am a multiple of 9. What number am I?

Exploring Division

Manipulatives

Use place-value blocks to model each pattern. Record the numbers as you complete each step.

1. 3)69
2. 2)26
3. 4)84
4. 2)36
5. 3)42

6. 2)30
7. 4)52
8. 5)55
9. 2)54
10. 3)72

Draw place-value materials to model each money amount.

11. $3.27

12. $1.78

13. $2.46

14. $4.12

VISUAL THINKING

Match each division number sentence with the correct model.

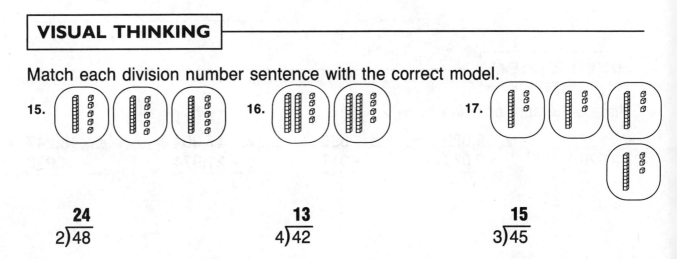

15.

16.

17.

$$\frac{24}{2)48}$$

$$\frac{13}{4)42}$$

$$\frac{15}{3)45}$$

Estimating Quotients

Ring the letter of the best estimate. Write the method
you used.

1. 3)‾175‾   a. 50   b. 60   c. 70   d. 75   _____

2. 4)‾243‾   a. 40   b. 70   c. 60   d. 80   _____

3. 2)‾178‾   a. 90   b. 80   c. 75   d. 78   _____

Estimate the quotient. Look for compatible numbers.

4. 2)‾107‾   5. 3)‾185‾   6. 4)‾158‾   7. 8)‾235‾   8. 7)‾148‾

9. 3)‾208‾   10. 5)‾403‾   11. 6)‾131‾   12. 4)‾321‾   13. 2)‾165‾

14. $275 \div 9 =$ _____   15. $426 \div 7 =$ _____   16. $356 \div 6 =$ _____

17. $555 \div 8 =$ _____   18. $809 \div 9 =$ _____   19. $348 \div 5 =$ _____

Mixed Applications

20. A theater has 238 seats. The
seats are arranged in 3 sections
of the same size. About how
many seats are in each section?

_____

21. A 117-minute film is recorded and
divided equally onto two large
reels. About how many minutes
of film does each reel contain?

_____

MIXED REVIEW

Estimate the sum or difference.

1.	2.	3.	4.	5.
897	9,000	386	47,904	18,247
− 528	+ 2,036	+ 917	+ 21,974	− 4,986

Problem Solving
Choose a Strategy

STRATEGIES	• Guess and Check • Make a Table • Act It Out • Draw a Picture • Work Backward • Find a Pattern • Write a Number Sentence

Choose a strategy and solve. Use the table for Exercises 5 and 6.

Complete the table for Exercises 1–4.

Number of Television Channels			
Programming	Total	Public	Pay
1. Educational	5		0
2. News	10	10	
3. Movies	22	7	
4. Community Service	25		2

5. What is the total number of public stations?

_____

6. How many more stations are public than pay?

_____

7. For $10 per month, one movie channel can be ordered. Each additional movie channel ordered costs $4. How much would 4 movie channels cost per month?

_____

8. One public community service channel shows the local weather every 5 minutes. How many times is the weather shown in one hour?

_____

9. Nancy watches 9 hours of news and 6 hours of movies each week. How many more hours of news than movies does Nancy watch?

_____

10. Ed watches 24 hours of television each week. He spends the same amount of time watching each type of programming. How many hours does Ed watch news?

_____

WRITER'S CORNER

11. Use the table above to write a word problem about television programming.

_____

Dividing Two-Digit Numbers

Write an X where the first digit in the quotient should be placed.

1. 6)30   2. 5)84   3. 9)75   4. 3)82   5. 8)58   6. 3)27

Find the quotient. Check by multiplying.

7. 3)51 Check: 8. 4)55 Check: 9. 6)82 Check: 10. 4)96 Check:

11. 4)87 Check: 12. 5)65 Check: 13. 3)89 Check: 14. 6)71 Check:

Mixed Applications

15. Benita is making a sign. She buys paints in 6 colors. Each can of paint costs $1.39. How much does Benita spend?

16. Benita wants to alternate the paint colors for each letter in her sign. The sign contains 84 letters. How many letters will she have of each color?

NUMBER SENSE

17. Follow the steps using your age. Then repeat the problem using ages of other people you know.

What is your answer every time? _____

START ⟶ Write your age ⟶ Add 3 ⟶ Multiply the sum by 3 ⟶
Subtract your age ⟶ Subtract 1 more ⟶ Divide by 2 ⟶
Subtract your age again ⟶ END

Dividing Three-Digit Numbers

Write an X where the first digit in the quotient should be placed.

1. 4)348   2. 5)712   3. 7)948   4. 4)678   5. 9)360

Find the quotient. Check by multiplying.

6. 3)254 Check: 7. 2)130 Check: 8. 6)737 Check: 9. 5)419 Check:

Mixed Applications

Gary works at a music store. He arranges tapes, records, and compact discs on shelves. Only one type of audio material is placed on a shelf. Complete the table Gary made. Then use it for Exercises 13 and 14.

Estimated Number of Audio Materials

	Audio Material	Total Number	Number of Shelves	About How Many On Each Shelf
10.	Records	487	6	
11.	Tapes	944	5	
12.	Compact discs	875	9	

13. Which type of audio material has the fewest items per shelf?

_____

14. If the tapes were evenly divided among 8 shelves, how many would be on each shelf?

_____

SOCIAL STUDIES CONNECTION

In a certain scale drawing, every length of 1 inch represents an actual length of 3 feet. Use division to find the length or height of each object in the scale drawing.

15. a fence 6 feet high _____ in.   16. a boat 99 feet long _____ in.

17. a tree 342 feet tall _____ in.   18. a bridge 186 feet long _____ in.

Zeros in the Quotient

Write an X where the first digit in the quotient should be placed.

1. 4)216

2. 8)578

3. 5)602

4. 8)824

5. 6)612

Estimate. Then find the quotient.

6. 7)722   Estimate: _____

7. 4)809   Estimate: _____

8. 8)859   Estimate: _____

Complete. Use mental math to find *n*.

9. If 600 ÷ 6 = 100,
   then 602 ÷ 6 = *n*.
   n = _____

10. If 300 ÷ 3 = 100,
    then 301 ÷ 3 = *n*.
    n = _____

11. If 800 ÷ 4 = 200,
    then 803 ÷ 4 = *n*.
    n = _____

Mixed Applications

12. Tami designs covers for record albums. She completes 4 covers a year. About how many days does Tami take to design 1 record cover?

_____

13. What is the greatest three-digit number that gives a two-digit quotient and a remainder of 1 when divided by 2?

_____

MIXED REVIEW

Find the quotient. Check by multiplying.

1. 22 ÷ 4 = _____

2. 25 ÷ 4 = _____

3. 51 ÷ 8 = _____

Estimate the quotient.

4. 5)42

5. 6)40

6. 9)48

7. 8)18

8. 7)50

Dividing with Money

Find the quotient. Check by multiplying.

1. 3)$2.79 Check:	2. 5)$8.50 Check:	3. 4)$8.16 Check:
4. 6)$5.22 Check:	5. 8)$6.32 Check:	6. 5)$6.00 Check:

7. $8.14 ÷ 2 = n
 	
n = _____
        Check:
	8. $5.44 ÷ 8 = n
	
	n = _____
	        Check:
		9. $8.05 ÷ 7 = n
		
		n = _____
		        Check:

Mixed Applications

10. Spudhouse has a special offer of 4 dinners for $9.72. How much is one dinner?

_____

11. An 8-ounce package of turkey costs $2.64. How much does the turkey cost per ounce?

_____

WRITER'S CORNER

12. Write step-by-step directions for solving a division problem involving money. Use words such as *quotient, dividend, dollars, dimes, pennies, dollar sign,* and *decimal point.*

_____

_____

Problem Solving
Choose the Method

Write which method you would use to solve the problem. Solve.

1. Mr. Wade collected $900 from the sale of a $3 magazine at his newsstand. How many issues did he sell?

   _____

2. Mr. Wade sells 85 copies of a magazine that sells for $1.25 a copy. How much does he collect from sales of the magazine?

   _____

Mixed Applications

Choose a method and solve.

3. Mr. Wade carries 3 more than 3 times as many different magazines as newspapers. He carries 85 different newspapers. How many different magazines does Mr. Wade carry?

   _____

4. Mr. Wade sells a total of about 942 papers a day. Does he sell more than 7,000 papers in a week?

   _____

5. Mr. Wade places news magazines in the middle of one shelf. Business magazines are beside news magazines. Cooking magazines are on the right end. Sports magazines are between news and cooking magazines. Where are the nature magazines?

   _____

6. Mr. Wade works for 5 straight hours when he opens his stand. After a 1-hour break, he works 6 hours and 15 minutes before closing at 6:10 P.M. What time does Mr. Wade open his stand?

   _____

VISUAL THINKING

7. Write a problem that could be solved using the picture.

   _____

   _____

Exploring Averages

Manipulatives

Use connecting cubes to explore finding the average. The data in the table tells how many photographs from several places Ana took. Let one connecting cube stand for one photograph.

Ana's Photographs	
Zoo	9
Family Picnic	6
Space Museum	7
Birthday party	10
School play	3

Use the table for Exercises 1–5.

1. How many stacks did you make?

_____

2. Write a number sentence to show how many cubes you used in all.

_____

3. Arrange the cubes in equal stacks. How many cubes are in each stack?

_____

4. What is the average number of photographs that Ana took of each place?

_____

5. Write a number sentence to show how you found your answer.

_____

SCIENCE CONNECTION

6. Three crews worked in a space station. They spent 29, 58, and 84 days in the space station. What was the average length of time the crews spent in the station? Write an addition number sentence and a division number sentence to show how you got the answer.

_____

Median, Range, and Average

Find the median, range, and average for each set of numbers.

1. 3, 10, 5 _____

2. 22, 42, 35 _____

3. 4, 11, 9, 6, 5 _____

4. 35, 26, 18, 25, 31 _____

5. 112, 64, 67, 79, 103 _____

6. 96, 120, 102, 95, 124, 101, 125 _____

Find the average for each set of test scores.

7. 83, 97, 100, 84, 76 _____

8. 89, 92, 75, 100, 98, 92 _____

Mixed Applications

9. Find the median, range, and average of the data in the graph.

_____

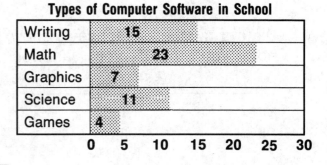

Types of Computer Software in School

Writing	15
Math	23
Graphics	7
Science	11
Games	4

0   5   10   15   20   25   30

SOCIAL STUDIES CONNECTION

10. Imagine that you work as a survey taker. You collect data by asking many people the same question. Survey 5 to 9 people on this question. Record your results in the chart.

About how many hours of television do you watch in one week?

Hours of TV Watched in One Week

Names								
Hours								

Find the median, range, and average number of hours of television watched in one week.

_____

Exploring Plane and Solid Figures

Look at these plane figures.

Which solid figure could you use to

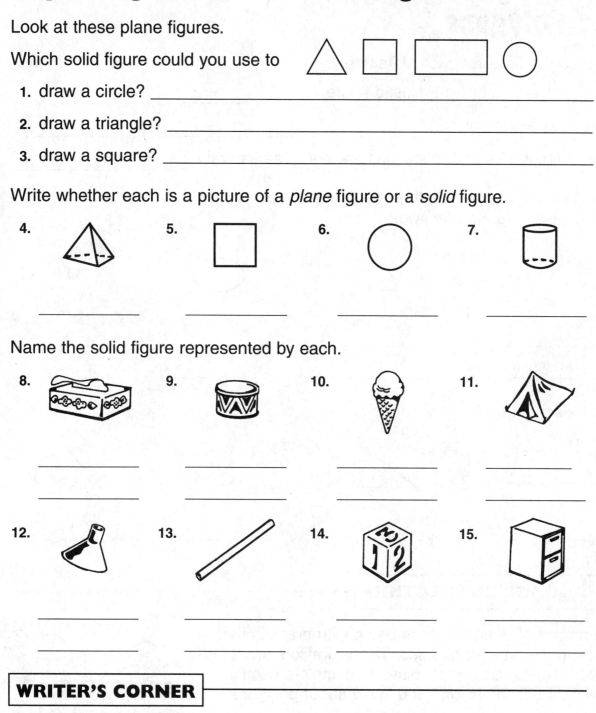

1. draw a circle? _____

2. draw a triangle? _____

3. draw a square? _____

Write whether each is a picture of a *plane* figure or a *solid* figure.

4. _____ 5. _____ 6. _____ 7. _____

Name the solid figure represented by each.

8. _____ 9. _____ 10. _____ 11. _____

12. _____ 13. _____ 14. _____ 15. _____

WRITER'S CORNER

16. Write a description of a solid figure. Ask a friend or family member to identify the figure from your description.

_____

_____

Exploring Plane Figures and Polygons

Write *true* or *false* for each statement.

1. A polygon is always a closed figure. _____

2. A square is a polygon. _____

3. Some squares and rectangles are not quadrilaterals. _____

Write *yes* or *no* to tell whether the figure is a polygon. Give a reason for your answer.

4.

5.

6.

7.

_____   _____   _____   _____

_____   _____   _____   _____

Name each figure.

8.

9.

10.

11.

_____   _____   _____   _____

LANGUAGE CONNECTION

The names of most polygons begin with prefixes that describe the number of sides. These prefixes are found in other words. Use prefix clues to complete each statement based on what you know about polygons.

12. An *octopus* has 8 legs, just as an _____

is a figure with _____ sides.

13. A *tricycle* has 3 wheels, just as a _____

is a figure with _____ sides.

Exploring Area

Draw a model for each area given. Use the grid.

1. 10 square units

2. 16 square units

3. 30 square units

Find the area in square units. Write a multiplication number sentence for Exercises 6 and 7.

4.

5.

6.

_____

_____

7.

_____

_____

_____

_____

8. Which of the four figures below have the same areas but different perimeters?

_____

9. Which of the four figures below have the same perimeters but different areas?

_____

A   B   C   D

SOCIAL STUDIES CONNECTION

Some states have shapes that are nearly rectangles. Use a calculator. Find the approximate areas of these states.

10.

Colorado

L: 600 km
W: 450 km   _____

11.

North Dakota

L: 540 km
W: 330 km   _____

Problem Solving
Multistep Problems

1. Raya rides 8 miles from her home to Spanish class. How many miles does Raya travel in 4 weeks if she travels to class and back once each week?

   _____

2. Raya rents a *Learning Spanish* tape for 4 days from the video store. The first day costs $2.72, and each additional day costs $1.50. What was the total cost of renting the tape?

   _____

3. Raya plans a 6-day trip to Mexico with her Spanish class. The cost is $65 per day for hotel and food, and $279 for air fare. What is the total cost of the trip?

   _____

4. While in Mexico, Raya takes lots of pictures. She uses 7 rolls of 36-photo film and 4 rolls of 24-photo film. How many photos does Raya take?

   _____

Mixed Applications

5. Raya's class took a tour of a Mexican museum. They arrived at the museum at 10:30 A.M. and left 5 hours 15 minutes later. At what time did they leave?

   _____

6. An enormous woven wall-hanging in the the museum was 16 feet wide and 50 feet tall. What was the area of the hanging?

   _____

SOCIAL STUDIES CONNECTION

The unit of currency, or money, in Mexico is the *peso*. About 9 pesos are equal to one United States dollar.

Raya gave each storekeeper 100 pesos. How many pesos did she receive in change from each purchase?

7.

   _____

8.

   _____

9.
   $7.00

   _____

100

Line Segments, Lines, and Rays

Identify each figure. Write *line segment, line, point,* or *ray.*

1. ●————————● 　　 2. ●————————→ 　　 3. ● 　　 4. ←————————→

_____ 　 _____ 　 _____ 　 _____

Draw each figure.

5. line *AB* 　　　　 6. ray *CD* 　　　　 7. line segment *EF*

Decide whether the figure is a line segment. Write *yes* or *no.*

8. ●————————→ 　 9. ●————————● 　 10. ←————————→ 　 11. ⬭

_____ 　 _____ 　 _____ 　 _____

Mixed Applications

12. Connect the endpoints in the diagram to make a closed figure. Find the perimeter and area of the figure.

Perimeter: _____ units

Area: _____ square unit

13. A 100-yard football field has markers drawn every ten yards, and at both ends. How many markers are drawn on the field? Complete the picture to prove your answer.

_____

14. What figure is formed inside the polygon if all of the possible line segments are drawn to connect the five points shown?

_____

Exploring Angles

Write whether each example is a *right,* an *acute,* or an *obtuse* angle.

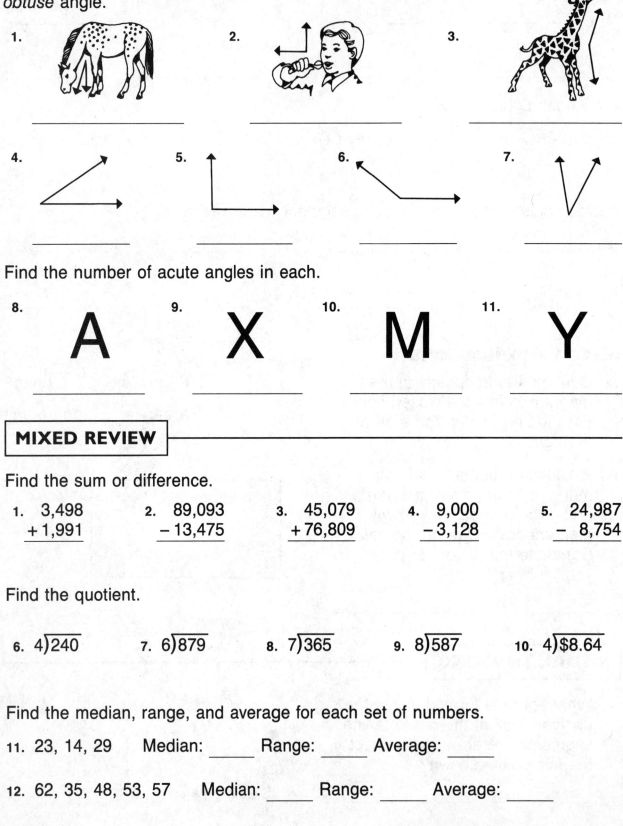

1.

_____

2.

_____

3.

_____

4.

_____

5.

_____

6.

_____

7.

_____

Find the number of acute angles in each.

8. **A**

_____

9. **X**

_____

10. **M**

_____

11. **Y**

_____

MIXED REVIEW

Find the sum or difference.

1. 3,498 + 1,991	2. 89,093 − 13,475	3. 45,079 + 76,809	4. 9,000 − 3,128	5. 24,987 − 8,754

Find the quotient.

6. 4)240   7. 6)879   8. 7)365   9. 8)587   10. 4)$8.64

Find the median, range, and average for each set of numbers.

11. 23, 14, 29   Median: _____   Range: _____   Average: _____

12. 62, 35, 48, 53, 57   Median: _____   Range: _____   Average: _____

Line Relationships

Write whether each picture suggests *intersecting lines*,
parallel lines, *perpendicular lines*, or *rays*.

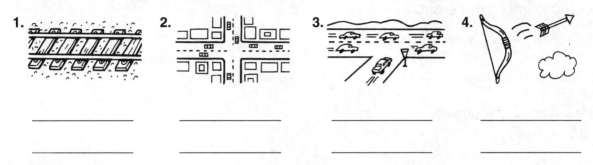

1. _____

2. _____

3. _____

4. _____

_____

_____

_____

_____

Draw the line segments that are described.

5. parallel

6. perpendicular

7. intersecting

Mixed Applications

8. What are the times of day when the hour hand is perpendicular to the minute hand and the minute hand points to the 12?

_____

9. Martha went ice skating one day for 3 hours and 25 minutes. She stopped at 5:15. What time did Martha begin to skate?

_____

Write your own definitions for parallel, perpendicular, and intersecting lines. Ask a family member or friend to identify the word for each definition as you read it aloud.

10. Parallel lines _____

_____

11. Perpendicular lines _____

_____

12. Intersecting lines _____

_____

Exploring Circles

Draw a circle. Use your centimeter ruler
to measure the radius and the diameter.
Label the points on the circle.

1. What is the name of your circle?

   _____

2. How many centimeters long is
   the radius?

   _____

3. How many centimeters long is
   the diameter?

   _____

Use the drawing for Exercises 4–6.

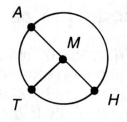

4. Name the center of this circle. _____

5. Name a radius. _____

6. Name a diameter. _____

Complete. Use the drawing for Exercises 7–11.

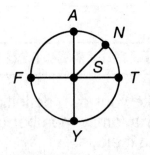

7. Line segment *FT* is a _____.

8. The center of the circle is _____.

9. Line segment *AS* is a _____.

10. Points *A* and *Y* are endpoints of a _____.

EVERYDAY MATH CONNECTION

11. Write how you would slice this pizza so that you
    could serve 8 people. Use words such as *circle*,
    diameter, *radius*, and *center* in your description.

    _____

    _____

Exploring Congruent and Similar Figures

Write whether each pair of figures is *congruent*, *similar*, or *both*.

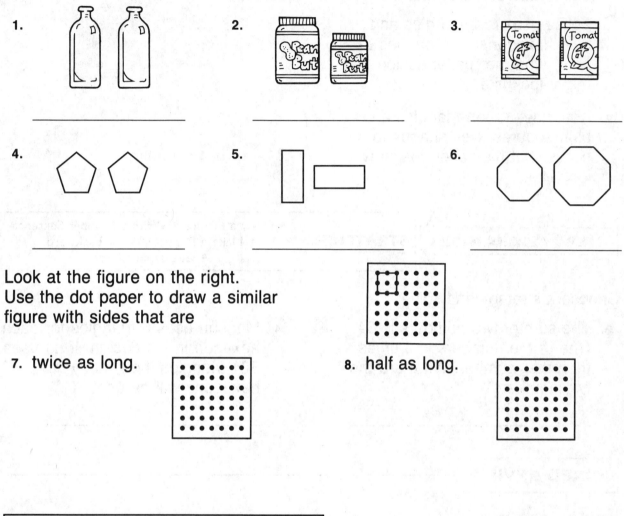

1. _____

2. _____

3. _____

4. _____

5. _____

6. _____

Look at the figure on the right.
Use the dot paper to draw a similar figure with sides that are

7. twice as long.

8. half as long.

SOCIAL STUDIES CONNECTION

9. Anne has a map of the United States in her social studies book. She also has a wall map of the United States. Are the two maps congruent, similar, both, or neither? Would a third map of the United States be similar or congruent to the first two? Explain.

_____

_____

_____

Problem-Solving Strategy
Make a Model

Tessa's family is making a wall mural. Each rectangular panel is made of hexagons, triangles, or squares.

1. Tessa uses red triangles and blue hexagons. Use shapes to show what her panel design might look like.

2. Ariel uses green triangles and blue squares. Use shapes to show what his panel design will look like.

Mixed Applications ➤ STRATEGIES
• Draw a Picture • Write a Number Sentence
• Make a Model • Work Backward
• Guess and Check

Choose a strategy and solve.

3. The sum of two numbers is 64. One of the numbers is 3 times the other number. What are the two numbers?

4. Manchu uses 6 triangles for each hexagon in his design. If he uses 324 triangles, how many hexagons will he use?

MIXED REVIEW

Identify each figure.

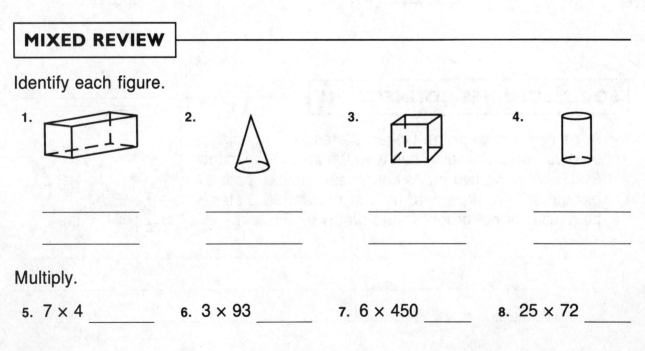

1.

2.

3.

4.

Multiply.

5. 7 × 4 _____

6. 3 × 93 _____

7. 6 × 450 _____

8. 25 × 72 _____

Symmetry

How many lines of symmetry does each figure have?

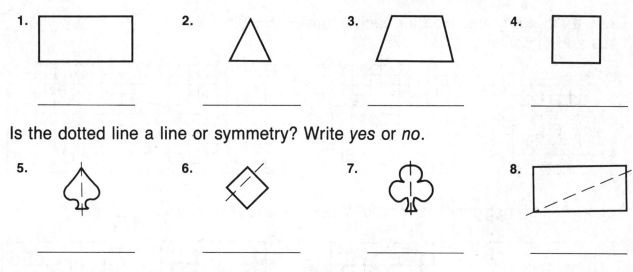

1. _____

2. _____

3. _____

4. _____

Is the dotted line a line or symmetry? Write *yes* or *no*.

5. _____

6. _____

7. _____

8. _____

Draw the other half of the figure to show that it has two symmetric parts.

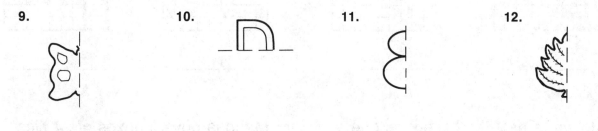

9.

10.

11.

12.

Mixed Applications

13. Name three things in your classroom that are symmetric.

    _____

    _____

    _____

14. Carmen has 78 photographs to put in her album. Each page of the album holds 6 photographs. How many pages will Carmen's photographs take up?

    _____

VISUAL THINKING

15. Imagine that you are building a house. You want the front of the house to have a vertical line of symmetry. It must have one door and three windows. Windows may have any shape. Draw a picture of the front of the house.

Exploring Slides, Flips, and Turns

Draw a flip, turn, and slide for each figure. Show flip lines and direction arrows.

1.

2.

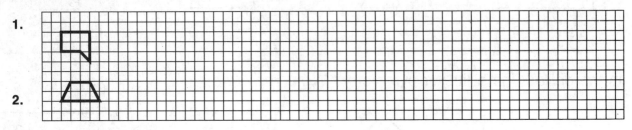

Tell how each polygon was moved. Write *flip, slide,* or *turn.*

3.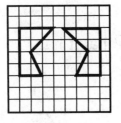

_____

4.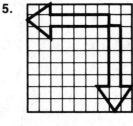

_____

5.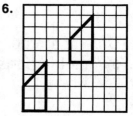

6.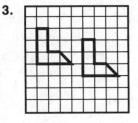

Solve.

7. Jo walks past the bakery on one side of Elm Street. How many turns must she make to be walking in the opposite direction on the other side of Elm Street?

_____

8. Miranda buys 5 boxes of 24 tiles to make a floor design. She uses all but 7 tiles. How many tiles does Miranda use for the floor design?

_____

EVERYDAY MATH CONNECTION

Use *flip, slide,* or *turn* to answer each question. Which motion do you use when you do each?

9. open a jar of peanut butter

_____

10. zip a jacket

_____

11. turn a page in a magazine

_____

12. screw in a lightbulb

_____

Solid Figures

Name the solid figure represented by each.

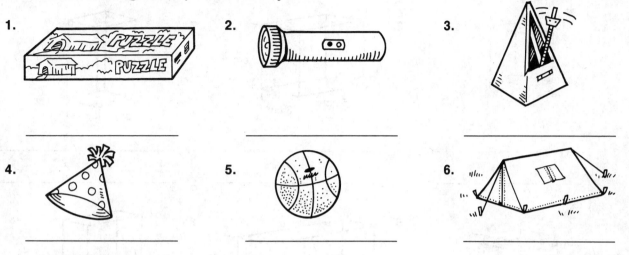

1. _____

2. _____

3. _____

4. _____

5. _____

6. _____

Name the solid figure that has

7. 4 flat faces. _____

8. 1 flat face. _____

9. 8 vertices. _____

10. 0 vertices. _____

11. 12 straight edges. _____

12. 6 straight edges. _____

13. 2 curved edges. _____

14. 1 curved face. _____

Mixed Applications

15. Frank keeps his button collection in a container that has two flat faces and a curved surface. What solid figure names the container?

    _____

16. A pilot flew 37,022 miles in May and 40,772 miles in June. In which month did he fly the greater number of miles?

    _____

LOGICAL REASONING

17. What two solid figures could you use to model a house with a roof? Draw a picture showing your model and write the names of the figures on the line below.

    _____

    _____

Exploring Volume

Write a multiplication sentence to find the volume of each.

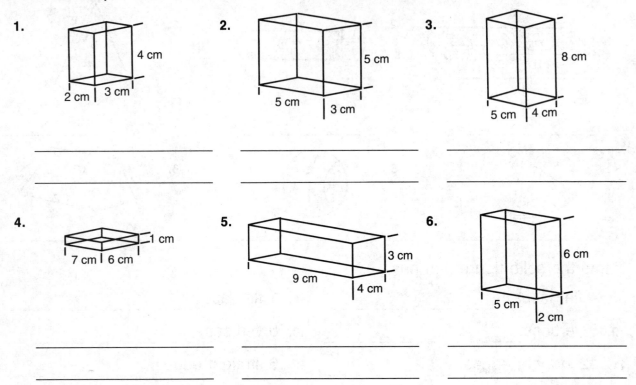

1. 4 cm, 2 cm, 3 cm

2. 5 cm, 5 cm, 3 cm

3. 8 cm, 5 cm, 4 cm

4. 1 cm, 7 cm, 6 cm

5. 3 cm, 9 cm, 4 cm

6. 6 cm, 5 cm, 2 cm

Complete this table for rectangular prisms.

	Length	Width	Height	Volume
7.	2 cm	4 cm	8 cm	
8.	3 cm	5 cm	2 cm	
9.	8 cm	3 cm	1 cm	
10.	4 cm		2 cm	24 cubic cm
11.		4 cm	4 cm	96 cubic cm

MATH CONNECTION

The small 3 in 6^3 is a special way to show the product of 3 sixes. Thus, $6^3 = 6 \times 6 \times 6 = 216$.

Find the value.

12. $2^3 =$ _____

13. $4^3 =$ _____

14. $3^3 =$ _____

15. $5^3 =$ _____

Connecting Geometry and Measurement

1. Sort the figures in the picture by drawing them in the table.

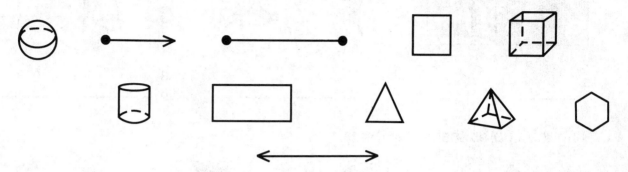

One-Dimensional	Two-Dimensional	Three-Dimensional

Solve.

2. For which type of figure are *square units* used to measure area?

_____

3. For which type of figure are *cubic units* used to measure volume?

_____

Tell whether you would use *units*, *square units*, or *cubic units* to measure each.

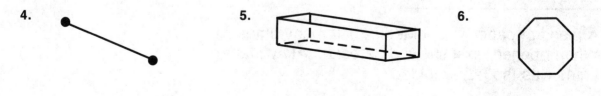

4. _____

5. _____

6.

Exploring Fractions

Write *part of a whole* or *part of a group* to describe
each example.

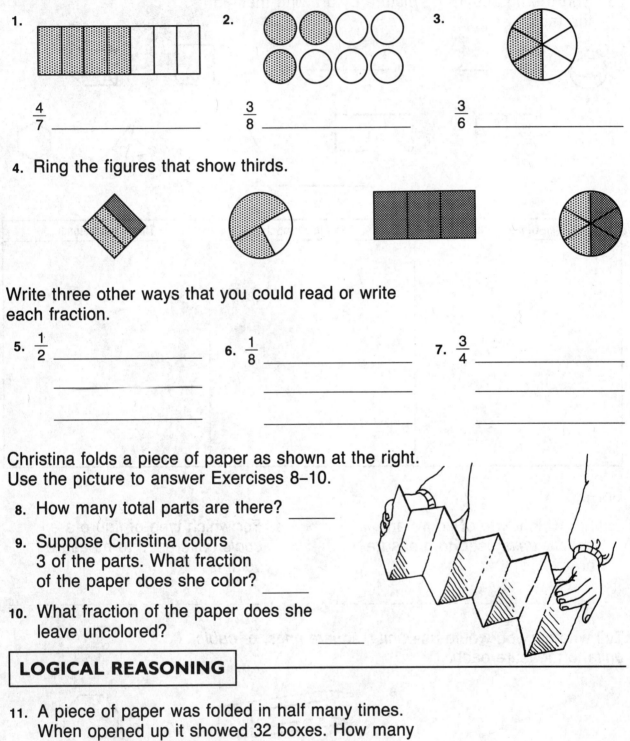

1.

$\frac{4}{7}$ _____

2.

$\frac{3}{8}$ _____

3.

$\frac{3}{6}$ _____

4. Ring the figures that show thirds.

Write three other ways that you could read or write
each fraction.

5. $\frac{1}{2}$ _____

6. $\frac{1}{8}$ _____

7. $\frac{3}{4}$ _____

_____   _____   _____

_____   _____   _____

Christina folds a piece of paper as shown at the right.
Use the picture to answer Exercises 8–10.

8. How many total parts are there? _____

9. Suppose Christina colors
3 of the parts. What fraction
of the paper does she color? _____

10. What fraction of the paper does she
leave uncolored? _____

LOGICAL REASONING

11. A piece of paper was folded in half many times.
When opened up it showed 32 boxes. How many
times was the paper folded?

_____

Fractions
Part of a Whole

Write a fraction for the shaded part.

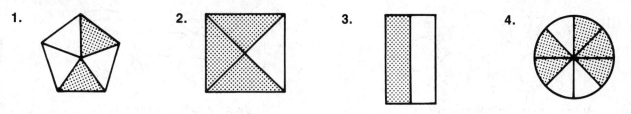

1.   2.   3.   4.

_____   _____   _____   _____

Use this rectangle to answer Exercises 5–7.

5. How much of the figure is shaded? _____

6. How much of the figure is not shaded? _____

7. How many sixths are in 1 whole? _____

Mixed Applications

8. Mrs. Ho cut an apple pie into 8 equal pieces. Ben ate 3 pieces. What fraction of the apple pie was not eaten?

_____

9. Mrs. Ho used 8 apples to make the pie. She cut each apple into 16 slices. How many slices of apple are in the pie?

_____

| **VISUAL THINKING** |

This number line is marked to show parts of the same length between 0 and 1.

Complete each number line.

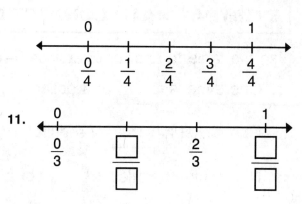

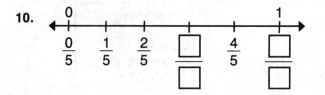

10.

11.

Fractions
Part of a Group

Write the fraction.

1.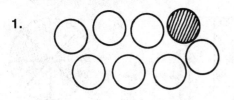

   What part is shaded? _____

2.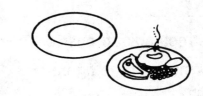

   What part has frogs? _____

3.

   What part is flying? _____

4.

   What part has food? _____

5. None of the five girls played volleyball.

   _____

6. All of the nine teachers watched the game.

   _____

Mixed Applications

7. Maria needs a total of 4 eggs in her muffin batter. She has already added 3 eggs. What fraction of eggs has she already added to the batter?

   _____

8. Maria bought flour for $3.98, eggs for $1.79, and milk for $1.59. How much change did she get from a ten-dollar bill?

   _____

EVERYDAY MATH CONNECTION

Use the table to answer Exercises 9–11.

9. One dime is _____ of a dollar.

10. One nickel is _____ of a dollar.

11. Ninety-nine pennies is _____ of a dollar.

Ways to Make $1.00
100 pennies
20 nickels
10 dimes
4 quarters
2 half-dollars

Exploring
Finding a Fraction of a Number

Use the pictures to help you complete Exercises 1–3.

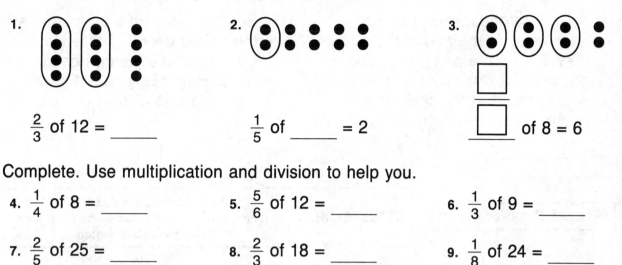

1. $\frac{2}{3}$ of 12 = _____

2. $\frac{1}{5}$ of _____ = 2

3. $\frac{\square}{\square}$ of 8 = 6

Complete. Use multiplication and division to help you.

4. $\frac{1}{4}$ of 8 = _____

5. $\frac{5}{6}$ of 12 = _____

6. $\frac{1}{3}$ of 9 = _____

7. $\frac{2}{5}$ of 25 = _____

8. $\frac{2}{3}$ of 18 = _____

9. $\frac{1}{8}$ of 24 = _____

10. Velma has 18 baseball cards. One half show National League players. How many of Velma's cards show National League players?

_____

11. Samuru has a collection of 15 model cars. Three-fifths are sports cars. How many of his cars are sports cars?

_____

12. Ramona has a collection of 80 stamps. One-fourth are British stamps. The rest are United States stamps. How many of Ramona's stamps are United States stamps?

_____

13. Brett collects rocks. His display case has 8 rows of rocks. There are 12 rocks in each row. How many rocks can Brett fit in his display case?

_____

CONSUMER CONNECTION

The hobby shop is having a sale on stamp albums.

$\frac{1}{3}$ of $15 = $5   You save $5.

Stamp Albums Regularly $15 NOW $\frac{1}{3}$ OFF!

Write the amount saved.

14. Regular Price: $9
    $\frac{1}{3}$ off _____

15. Regular Price: $24
    $\frac{1}{2}$ off _____

16. Regular Price: $20
    $\frac{2}{5}$ off _____

Problem-Solving Strategy
Act It Out

Solve each problem by acting it out.

1. Amy, Sharonda, and Juan had a bake sale. At the end of the day they shared the profit of 1 five-dollar bill, 2 one-dollar bills, 6 quarters, and 1 nickel. How much did each person receive?

_____

2. Sharonda set up 3 tables to sell the baked goods. There were 6 cakes and 6 pies on each table. How many baked goods were there in all?

_____

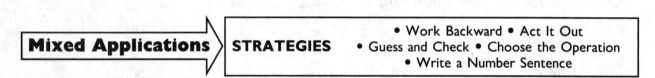

Mixed Applications ⟩ **STRATEGIES** • Work Backward • Act It Out • Guess and Check • Choose the Operation • Write a Number Sentence

Choose a strategy and solve.

3. Ted went to the bake sale 20 minutes after it started. He arrived at the bake sale at 11:35 A.M. What time did the bake sale start?

_____

4. Amy folded a napkin in half several times. When she opened it up, it showed 8 squares. How many times did Amy fold the napkin?

_____

MIXED REVIEW

Ring the polygon that is congruent to the first polygon in the row. Then write how many lines of symmetry each figure has.

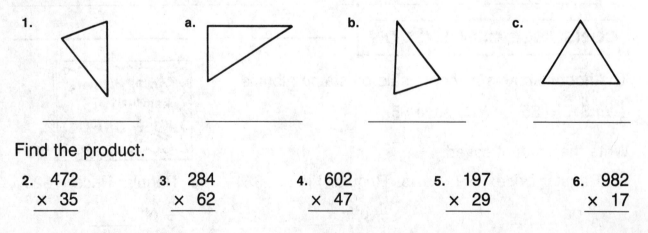

1.   a.   b.   c.

_____   _____   _____   _____

Find the product.

2. 472   3. 284   4. 602   5. 197   6. 982
   × 35   × 62   × 47   × 29   × 17

116

Exploring Equivalent Fractions

Complete these equivalent fractions. Use fraction bars
or counters to help you.

1. $\dfrac{1}{3} = \dfrac{\boxed{}}{6}$
   2. $\dfrac{1}{2} = \dfrac{\boxed{}}{4}$
   3. $\dfrac{3}{4} = \dfrac{\boxed{}}{8}$
   4. $\dfrac{3}{9} = \dfrac{\boxed{}}{3}$

Look at the first figure in each exercise. Then ring the
figure that shows a fraction equivalent to the first figure.

5.

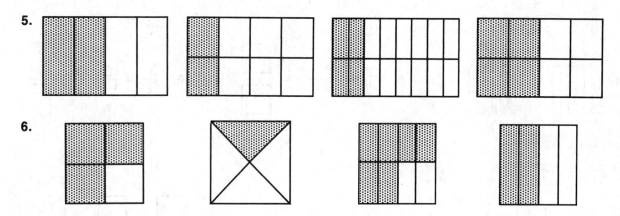

6.

Write two equivalent fractions for each.

7. $\dfrac{1}{4}$ _____
   8. $\dfrac{1}{5}$ _____
   9. $\dfrac{2}{3}$ _____
   10. $\dfrac{3}{8}$ _____

11. Alex eats $\dfrac{2}{8}$ of a muffin. Jed eats
$\dfrac{1}{4}$ of the same muffin. Who eats
more?

_____

12. Lena uses $\dfrac{1}{4}$ of a dozen eggs to
make pancakes. How many eggs
does she use?

_____

VISUAL THINKING

Write four equivalent fractions for each figure.

13.

14.

_____   _____

Fractions
Simplest Form

Complete.

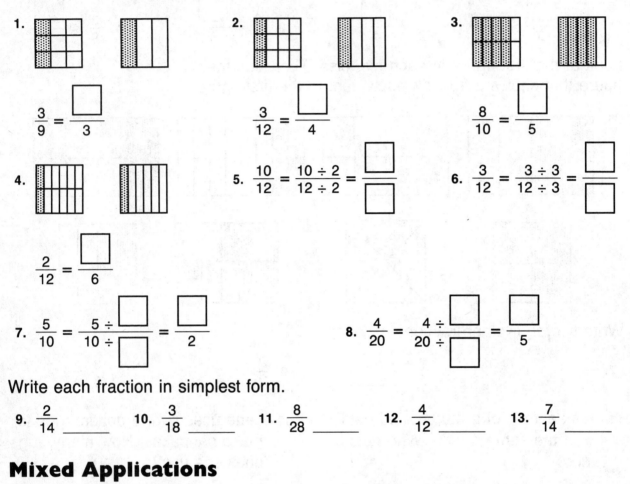

1. $\dfrac{3}{9} = \dfrac{\Box}{3}$

2. $\dfrac{3}{12} = \dfrac{\Box}{4}$

3. $\dfrac{8}{10} = \dfrac{\Box}{5}$

4. $\dfrac{2}{12} = \dfrac{\Box}{6}$

5. $\dfrac{10}{12} = \dfrac{10 \div 2}{12 \div 2} = \dfrac{\Box}{\Box}$

6. $\dfrac{3}{12} = \dfrac{3 \div 3}{12 \div 3} = \dfrac{\Box}{\Box}$

7. $\dfrac{5}{10} = \dfrac{5 \div \Box}{10 \div \Box} = \dfrac{\Box}{2}$

8. $\dfrac{4}{20} = \dfrac{4 \div \Box}{20 \div \Box} = \dfrac{\Box}{5}$

Write each fraction in simplest form.

9. $\dfrac{2}{14}$ _____

10. $\dfrac{3}{18}$ _____

11. $\dfrac{8}{28}$ _____

12. $\dfrac{4}{12}$ _____

13. $\dfrac{7}{14}$ _____

Mixed Applications

14. It takes Brian 40 minutes to bake a casserole. In simplest form, what part of an hour is 40 minutes?

15. Of the 24 hours in each day, Kisha spends $\frac{1}{3}$ of them sleeping. How many hours does she sleep?

_____

_____

MIXED REVIEW

Find each answer.

1. 38×27

2. $3{,}842 + 628$

3. $3\overline{)167}$

4. $7{,}623 - 1{,}906$

5. $9\overline{)\$0.45}$

Problem Solving
Choose a Strategy

STRATEGIES	• Write a Number Sentence • Act It Out • Work Backward • Guess and Check • Draw a Picture • Analyze Data to Make Decisions

1. Mr. Rodriguez plants a row of red flowers, then a row of blue flowers, and then a row of yellow flowers. He follows this pattern as he keeps on planting. What color are the flowers in the seventh row?

   _____

2. In a carton of 24 begonias, $\frac{3}{4}$ of them are red. The rest are white. How many begonias are white?

   _____

3. Joe watered plants for 7 hours. He watered for 3 more hours in the morning than in the afternoon. How long did he water in the morning and in the afternoon?

   _____

Mixed Applications

The manager of the garden shop made a graph to show the change in pottery sales over a 4-month period. Use the graph to answer Exercises 4–5.

4. During which month were the most pots sold?

   _____

5. How many more pots were sold in September than in November?

   _____

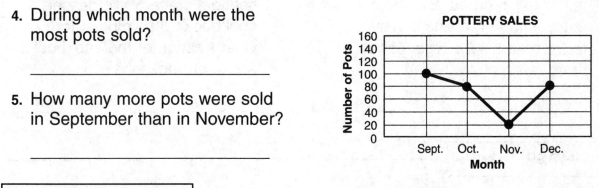

POTTERY SALES

WRITER'S CORNER

6. Use the information in the pottery-sales graph to write one problem.

   _____

   _____

Comparing Fractions

Write the fraction for each figure. Then compare
using $<$, $>$, or $=$.

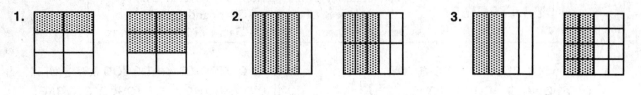

1. _____   2. _____   3. _____

Write *like* or *unlike* to describe each pair of fractions.
Then compare using $<$, $>$, or $=$. You may use fraction
bars to help you.

4. $\frac{1}{4}$ ◯ $\frac{2}{4}$ _____

5. $\frac{1}{2}$ ◯ $\frac{1}{4}$ _____

6. $\frac{4}{10}$ ◯ $\frac{9}{10}$ _____

7. $\frac{4}{5}$ ◯ $\frac{3}{5}$ _____

8. $\frac{2}{6}$ ◯ $\frac{2}{3}$ _____

9. $\frac{2}{4}$ ◯ $\frac{2}{6}$ _____

Use equivalent fractions to help you place each set in
order from least to greatest.

10. $\frac{6}{10}$, $\frac{4}{10}$, $\frac{9}{10}$ _____

11. $\frac{1}{2}$, $\frac{5}{6}$, $\frac{1}{6}$, $\frac{2}{3}$ _____

Mixed Applications

12. Ming Lei used $\frac{2}{3}$ cup of raisins
in her raisin bread. Elizabeth
used $\frac{5}{8}$ cup of raisins in her
raisin bread. Which girl used
more raisins?

_____

13. Of the 20 cookbooks in the
school library, 5 are dessert
cookbooks. In simplest form,
what fraction of the cookbooks
are about desserts?

_____

NUMBER SENSE

Compare. Write $<$, $>$, or $=$.

14. $\frac{1}{2}$ of 4 ◯ $\frac{1}{3}$ of 6

15. $\frac{1}{3}$ of 12 ◯ $\frac{1}{2}$ of 10

16. $\frac{5}{7}$ of 7 ◯ $\frac{1}{3}$ of 6

17. $\frac{1}{4}$ of 8 ◯ $\frac{1}{2}$ of 6

Exploring Mixed Numbers

Write a mixed number for each picture.

1.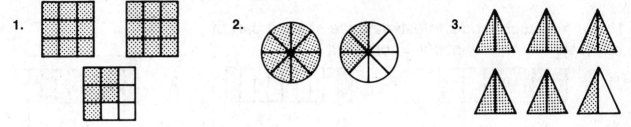

2.

3.

_____   _____   _____

Write each fraction as a mixed number. You may use your fraction circles to help you.

4. $\frac{11}{2}$ _____   5. $\frac{15}{7}$ _____   6. $\frac{14}{9}$ _____   7. $\frac{13}{4}$ _____   8. $\frac{10}{3}$ _____

9. Shelly used $\frac{10}{3}$ cups of noodles to make a tuna-noodle dish. How many cups of noodles did she use? Write the answer as a mixed number.

_____

10. Shelly also used $\frac{7}{2}$ cans of tuna in the tuna-noodle dish. How many cans of tuna did she use? Write the answer as a mixed number.

_____

11. Shelly paid $5.95 for 4 cans of tuna and a bag of noodles. Each can of tuna cost $1.29. How much did the noodles cost?

_____

12. A cup holds 8 ounces of liquid. Shelly used 30 ounces of milk to make some biscuits. How many cups did she use?

_____

LOGICAL REASONING

Complete the pattern.

13. $\frac{1}{2}$, 1, $1\frac{1}{2}$, _____ , _____ , _____ , _____

14. $\frac{2}{3}$, 1, $1\frac{1}{3}$, _____ , _____ , _____ , _____

15. $\frac{4}{7}$, 1, $1\frac{3}{7}$, _____ , _____ , _____ , _____

Exploring
Estimating Fractions

Use the fraction model to estimate the shaded part of each. Write *about 0, about $\frac{1}{2}$,* or *about 1.*

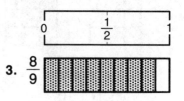

1. $\frac{4}{6}$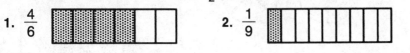

2. $\frac{1}{9}$

3. $\frac{8}{9}$

_____ _____ _____

Use the model above to estimate each. Draw pictures to show your estimate. Write *about 0, about $\frac{1}{2}$,* or *about $1\frac{1}{2}$.*

4. $\frac{8}{9} + \frac{11}{12}$

5. $\frac{7}{10} + \frac{10}{12}$

6. $\frac{2}{8} + \frac{5}{6}$

7. $\frac{1}{3} + \frac{1}{6}$

_____ _____ _____ _____

8. Awan has just completed the 7th lap in a swim meet. There are 15 laps in all. Has the meet just started, is it close to halfway, or is it almost over?

_____

9. Jason swam in 8 out of 9 meets. Becky swam in 4 out of 9 meets. Who swam in about one-half of the meets?

_____

LOGICAL REASONING

10. Write the numerator or denominator so the fraction is close to $\frac{1}{2}$.

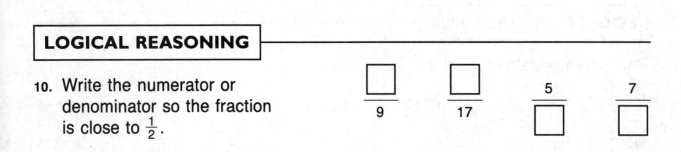

Exploring Adding Fractions with Like Denominators

Use fraction pieces to find the sum. You may write the sum in simplest form.

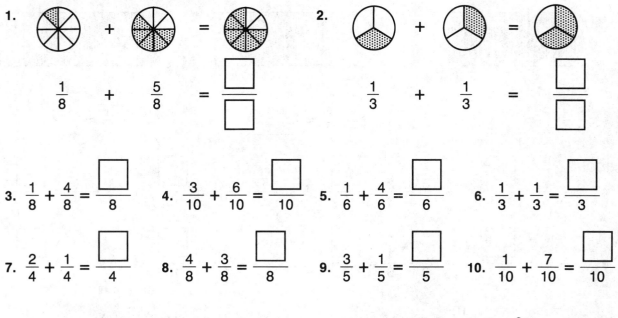

1. $\frac{1}{8} + \frac{5}{8} = \dfrac{\boxed{}}{\boxed{}}$

2. $\frac{1}{3} + \frac{1}{3} = \dfrac{\boxed{}}{\boxed{}}$

3. $\frac{1}{8} + \frac{4}{8} = \dfrac{\boxed{}}{8}$

4. $\frac{3}{10} + \frac{6}{10} = \dfrac{\boxed{}}{10}$

5. $\frac{1}{6} + \frac{4}{6} = \dfrac{\boxed{}}{6}$

6. $\frac{1}{3} + \frac{1}{3} = \dfrac{\boxed{}}{3}$

7. $\frac{2}{4} + \frac{1}{4} = \dfrac{\boxed{}}{4}$

8. $\frac{4}{8} + \frac{3}{8} = \dfrac{\boxed{}}{8}$

9. $\frac{3}{5} + \frac{1}{5} = \dfrac{\boxed{}}{5}$

10. $\frac{1}{10} + \frac{7}{10} = \dfrac{\boxed{}}{10}$

11. A scout troop hiked along a trail. The scouts hiked $\frac{2}{8}$ of the way on the first day and $\frac{3}{8}$ of the way on the second day. What part of the trail did they hike?

_____

12. Of the scout troop, $\frac{3}{12}$ slept in one tent and $\frac{4}{12}$ slept in another. The rest slept in a cabin. What part of the troop slept in tents?

_____

NUMBER SENSE

Write the missing addend.

13. $\frac{4}{5} + $ _____ $= 1$

14. $\frac{2}{3} + $ _____ $= 1$

15. $\frac{4}{10} + $ _____ $= 1$

Exploring Subtracting Fractions with Like Denominators

Use fraction pieces to find the difference.
You may write the difference in simplest form.

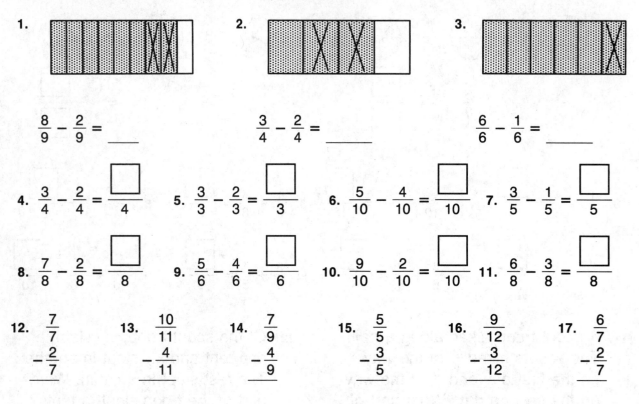

1. $\dfrac{8}{9} - \dfrac{2}{9} =$ _____

2. $\dfrac{3}{4} - \dfrac{2}{4} =$ _____

3. $\dfrac{6}{6} - \dfrac{1}{6} =$ _____

4. $\dfrac{3}{4} - \dfrac{2}{4} = \dfrac{\square}{4}$

5. $\dfrac{3}{3} - \dfrac{2}{3} = \dfrac{\square}{3}$

6. $\dfrac{5}{10} - \dfrac{4}{10} = \dfrac{\square}{10}$

7. $\dfrac{3}{5} - \dfrac{1}{5} = \dfrac{\square}{5}$

8. $\dfrac{7}{8} - \dfrac{2}{8} = \dfrac{\square}{8}$

9. $\dfrac{5}{6} - \dfrac{4}{6} = \dfrac{\square}{6}$

10. $\dfrac{9}{10} - \dfrac{2}{10} = \dfrac{\square}{10}$

11. $\dfrac{6}{8} - \dfrac{3}{8} = \dfrac{\square}{8}$

12. $\begin{array}{r} \dfrac{7}{7} \\ -\dfrac{2}{7} \\ \hline \end{array}$

13. $\begin{array}{r} \dfrac{10}{11} \\ -\dfrac{4}{11} \\ \hline \end{array}$

14. $\begin{array}{r} \dfrac{7}{9} \\ -\dfrac{4}{9} \\ \hline \end{array}$

15. $\begin{array}{r} \dfrac{5}{5} \\ -\dfrac{3}{5} \\ \hline \end{array}$

16. $\begin{array}{r} \dfrac{9}{12} \\ -\dfrac{3}{12} \\ \hline \end{array}$

17. $\begin{array}{r} \dfrac{6}{7} \\ -\dfrac{2}{7} \\ \hline \end{array}$

18. Elena had $\dfrac{5}{6}$ of a box of pancake mix. She used $\dfrac{4}{6}$ of the box to make pancakes for breakfast. How much of the pancake mix was left?

_____

19. Elena had $\dfrac{4}{5}$ of a pitcher of orange juice. Her family drank $\dfrac{3}{5}$ of a pitcher of the juice. Was there close to no orange juice, $\dfrac{1}{2}$ pitcher, or a whole pitcher left?

_____

NUMBER SENSE

20. Tom subtracted a fraction from $\dfrac{11}{12}$. The answer in simplest form was $\dfrac{1}{2}$. What fraction did he subtract?

_____

Problem-Solving Strategy
Make a Model

Make a model to solve.

1. A spinner has 12 equal sections. Two sections are red, 4 sections are yellow, 4 sections are blue, and 2 sections are green. What two colors together cover more than $\frac{1}{2}$ of the spinner?

   _____

2. A quilt is made from panels of fabric. One third of the panels are made from a plaid fabric, and one fourth of the panels are made from a flower print fabric. About how much of the quilt is plaid or a flower print?

   _____

Mixed Applications > **STRATEGIES** • Work Backward • Write a Number Sentence • Act It Out • Guess and Check

Choose a strategy and solve.

3. Suki bought a camera for $38.95 and film for $8.99. After these purchases she had $12.56 left. How much money did Suki have before her purchases?

   _____

4. Lars set up 4 tables for the book fair. He put 5 fiction books and 5 nonfiction books on each table. How many books did Lars display in all?

   _____

MIXED REVIEW

Find the difference.

1.	2.	3.	4.	5.
11	62	47	273	821
− 2	− 19	− 33	− 61	− 442

Complete to write equivalent fractions.

6. $\frac{1}{3} = \frac{\boxed{}}{6}$

7. $\frac{1}{2} = \frac{\boxed{}}{6}$

8. $\frac{3}{4} = \frac{\boxed{}}{12}$

9. $\frac{6}{9} = \frac{\boxed{}}{3}$

Exploring
Finding a Common Denominator

Use fraction pieces to help you find the
common denominator.

1. $\frac{2}{5}$ and $\frac{7}{10}$ _____

2. $\frac{2}{3}$ and $\frac{5}{6}$ _____

3. $\frac{1}{2}$ and $\frac{3}{4}$ _____

4. $\frac{1}{6}$ and $\frac{5}{12}$ _____

5. $\frac{1}{3}$ and $\frac{4}{9}$ _____

6. $\frac{3}{8}$ and $\frac{1}{4}$ _____

Mixed Applications

7. Samantha and her friend took
turns mowing the lawn. Samantha
mowed $\frac{4}{6}$ of the lawn and later
$\frac{1}{6}$ of the lawn. How much of the
lawn did Samantha mow in all?

_____

8. Bianca watered the lawn for $\frac{1}{3}$
hour in the afternoon and $\frac{2}{3}$ hour
in the evening. What fraction of
an hour did Bianca spend
watering the lawn? How many
minutes is this?

_____

VISUAL THINKING

On each clock face draw hands so that you can shade
in a region that matches the given fraction. Under each
clock face, write the time. For example, 5:00 could
represent $\frac{5}{12}$ or $\frac{7}{12}$ depending on which region you
shade.

9. $\frac{1}{2}$

10. $\frac{1}{3}$

11. $\frac{1}{4}$

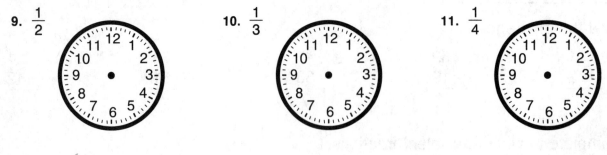

_____   _____   _____

Adding and Subtracting with Unlike Denominators

Complete. Use fraction pieces to help you.

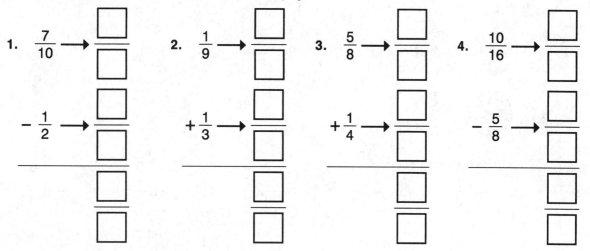

1. $\frac{7}{10}$ →
    $-\frac{1}{2}$ →

2. $\frac{1}{9}$ →
    $+\frac{1}{3}$ →

3. $\frac{5}{8}$ →
    $+\frac{1}{4}$ →

4. $\frac{10}{16}$ →
    $-\frac{5}{8}$ →

Mixed Applications

5. Alan is making a pineapple delight for dessert. He needs $\frac{3}{4}$ cup of pineapple. He has $\frac{1}{2}$ cup of pineapple. How many cups of pineapple does he still need?

_____

6. Alan uses $\frac{1}{4}$ cup of walnuts to make nutbread and $\frac{3}{8}$ cup to make the pineapple delight. How many cups of walnuts does he use in all?

_____

EVERYDAY MATH CONNECTION

7. Umeko has only a $\frac{1}{4}$-cup measuring spoon. Complete the table to tell how many times Umeko must fill the measuring spoon to get the correct amount of flour.

Amount of flour needed	$\frac{1}{2}$ cup	1 cup	$1\frac{1}{4}$ cups	2 cups	$3\frac{1}{2}$ cups	$5\frac{3}{4}$ cups
Number of spoonfuls						

Adding and Subtracting Mixed Numbers

Find the sum or difference. You may write your answer in simplest form.

1. 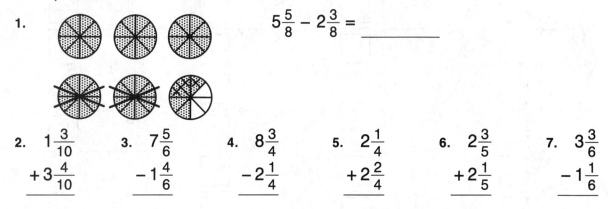 $5\frac{5}{8} - 2\frac{3}{8} =$ _____

2. $\begin{array}{r} 1\frac{3}{10} \\ +\ 3\frac{4}{10} \\ \hline \end{array}$

3. $\begin{array}{r} 7\frac{5}{6} \\ -\ 1\frac{4}{6} \\ \hline \end{array}$

4. $\begin{array}{r} 8\frac{3}{4} \\ -\ 2\frac{1}{4} \\ \hline \end{array}$

5. $\begin{array}{r} 2\frac{1}{4} \\ +\ 2\frac{2}{4} \\ \hline \end{array}$

6. $\begin{array}{r} 2\frac{3}{5} \\ +\ 2\frac{1}{5} \\ \hline \end{array}$

7. $\begin{array}{r} 3\frac{3}{6} \\ -\ 1\frac{1}{6} \\ \hline \end{array}$

Mixed Applications

Use the table to answer Exercises 8–9.

Bike Trails in Bamboo Park

Trail	Trail Length (miles)
Cherry Trail	$1\frac{1}{8}$
Apple Trail	$2\frac{5}{8}$
Elm Trail	$\frac{6}{8}$
Oak Trail	$3\frac{7}{8}$
Maple Trail	$2\frac{4}{8}$

8. Emilia rides her bicycle along Elm Trail and Cherry Trail. How far does Emilia ride in all?

_____

9. How much longer is Apple Trail than Maple Trail?

_____

SPORTS CONNECTION

10. A $2\frac{2}{3}$-mile bicycle race is held on a $\frac{1}{3}$-mile track. How many times must the racers go around the track to complete the race?

_____

128

Connecting Fractions and Measurement

Use a customary ruler to measure each to the nearest unit. Use $\frac{1}{2}$ inch, $\frac{1}{4}$ inch, or $\frac{1}{8}$ inch.

1.

_____

2.

_____

Name an object that measures about

3. 3 inches long. _____

4. $\frac{3}{4}$ inch wide. _____

Mixed Applications

5. Manuel made a square vegetable garden. Each side is $12\frac{1}{2}$ feet long. What is the perimeter of the vegetable garden?

   _____

6. It took Manuel 10 minutes to weed his garden, 15 minutes to fertilize, and 20 minutes to water his garden. For what part of an hour did Manuel work in his garden?

   _____

NUMBER SENSE

Estimate the length of each object. Then measure each. Find the difference between the estimate and the measurement. Complete the table.

	Object	Estimate	Measure	Difference
7.	Your middle finger			
8.	Your math book			
9.	Your shoe			

129

Problem Solving
Choose a Strategy

Mixed Applications → STRATEGIES   • Draw a Picture • Guess and Check
• Make an Organized List • Use Estimation

Choose a strategy. Solve.

1. Use the digits 2, 4, 6, and 8. List all the four-digit numbers you can make with 4 in the tens place.

_____

_____

2. An automobile maker offers seats in vinyl, leather, or cloth. Each type of seat is available in black, blue, or gray. How many seat choices are there?

_____

3. Ron and Skip went out for lunch. Ron spent $4.59 and Skip spent $5.17. Did they spend more or less than $10.00?

_____

4. Ayita has 40 stamps in her collection. There are 3 times as many British stamps as United States stamps. How many British stamps does Ayita have?

_____

5. Six brothers are lining up in order from the tallest to the shortest. Diego is taller than John. Dan is shorter than John but taller than Bob. Bob is taller than Geraldo. Jorge is the tallest. In what order should the brothers line up?

_____

6. A restaurant offers a choice of peas, carrots, or corn with any of the 4 main courses. The main courses available are chicken, pork, beef, and fish. How many dinner choices are there?

_____

WRITER'S CORNER

7. Write a problem that can be solved by using an organized list.

_____

_____

Exploring Probability

Look at the spinner. Find the probability of landing on

1. green. _____

2. yellow. _____

3. blue. _____

4. red. _____

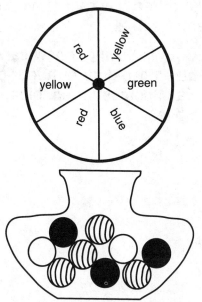

Look at the jar. Find the probability of picking a

5. black marble. _____

6. striped marble. _____

7. white marble. _____

8. A bag contains 10 marbles. There are 5 red marbles, 2 green marbles, and 3 blue marbles. If you pick a marble without looking, would you be more likely to get a red or a blue marble?

_____

9. Ted has a nickel, 5 quarters, and 2 dimes in his pocket. Which type of coin is he most likely to pull out of his pocket? Which type of coin is he least likely to pull out of his pocket?

_____

10. A jar contains 3 red marbles, 2 blue marbles, and 1 black marble. What is the probability of picking a blue marble?

_____

11. A spinner has 5 equal sections marked with the numbers 1 through 5. What is the probability of landing on an odd number?

_____

LOGICAL REASONING

12. The winner of the Crafts Fair Raffle will be the person whose name is drawn from among 100 name cards. The probability of a fourth grader winning is $\frac{1}{20}$. How many of the cards have the name of a fourth grader?

_____

Listing All Possibilities

Make a tree diagram of all possible combinations for Exercises 1–2.

1. Cora is buying a new car. She can buy a two-door or a four-door car. Each comes in red, blue, green, or white.

2. Blake wants to order a plate of pasta and salad. He can choose from 2 types of pasta and 3 types of salad.

Mixed Applications

3. Rosa mixed $1\frac{1}{4}$ quarts of cranberry juice with $1\frac{3}{4}$ quarts of apple juice. How much juice did she make in all?

4. Etu picked $1\frac{1}{3}$ bushels of grapes. Rosa picked $\frac{8}{6}$ bushels of grapes. Who picked more grapes?

MIXED REVIEW

Write each fraction in simplest form.

1. $\frac{2}{12}$ _____   2. $\frac{3}{18}$ _____   3. $\frac{7}{28}$ _____   4. $\frac{10}{24}$ _____   5. $\frac{8}{16}$ _____

Add or subtract. Write the sum in simplest form.

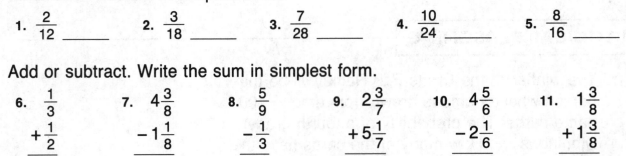

6. $\frac{1}{3}$
$+\frac{1}{2}$

7. $4\frac{3}{8}$
$-1\frac{1}{8}$

8. $\frac{5}{9}$
$-\frac{1}{3}$

9. $2\frac{3}{7}$
$+5\frac{1}{7}$

10. $4\frac{5}{6}$
$-2\frac{1}{6}$

11. $1\frac{3}{8}$
$+1\frac{3}{8}$

Exploring Decimals

Make a model for each decimal. Then write each decimal in words.

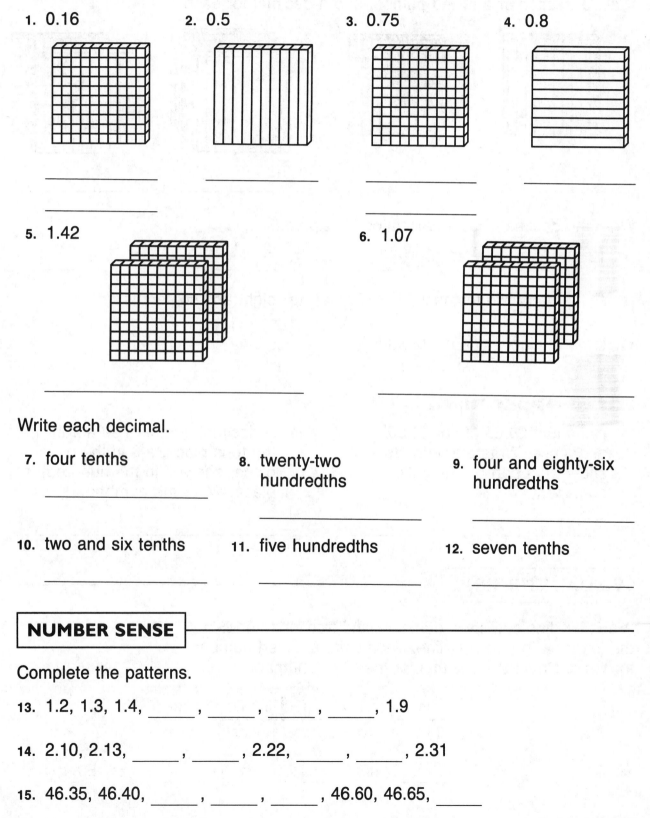

1. 0.16

_____

2. 0.5

_____

3. 0.75

_____

4. 0.8

_____

5. 1.42

_____

6. 1.07

_____

Write each decimal.

7. four tenths

_____

8. twenty-two hundredths

_____

9. four and eighty-six hundredths

_____

10. two and six tenths

_____

11. five hundredths

_____

12. seven tenths

_____

NUMBER SENSE

Complete the patterns.

13. 1.2, 1.3, 1.4, _____, _____, _____, _____, 1.9

14. 2.10, 2.13, _____, _____, 2.22, _____, _____, 2.31

15. 46.35, 46.40, _____, _____, _____, 46.60, 46.65, _____

Problem Solving
Choose a Strategy

Write a fraction or a mixed number and a decimal for each.

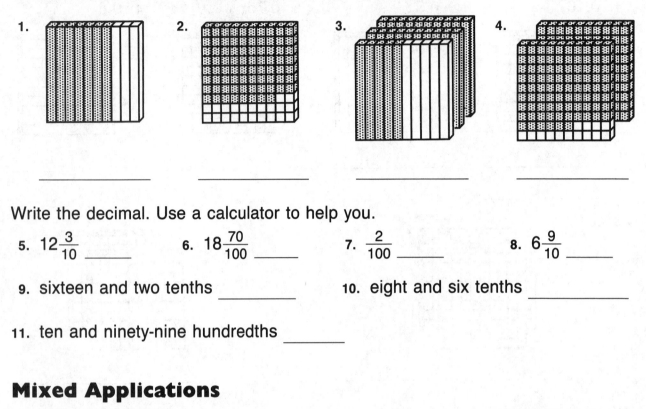

1.

2.

3.

4.

_____   _____   _____   _____

Write the decimal. Use a calculator to help you.

5. $12\frac{3}{10}$ _____

6. $18\frac{70}{100}$ _____

7. $\frac{2}{100}$ _____

8. $6\frac{9}{10}$ _____

9. sixteen and two tenths _____

10. eight and six tenths _____

11. ten and ninety-nine hundredths _____

Mixed Applications

12. Ilya spent $0.65 of her $1.00 allowance. Write a fraction to show what part of the dollar she spent.

13. A decimal number has a 2 in the tens place, a 6 in the ones place, and a 7 in the hundredths place. Write the number.

_____   _____

VISUAL THINKING

A number line can show decimals and fractions. Find the letter on the number line. Then write a mixed number for the decimal or a decimal for the mixed number.

```
  3    A  3 2/10   3 3/10  3 4/10   C  3 6/10  3 7/10  3 8/10   E  3 4/10
  <———|———|———|———|———|———|———|———|———|———|———>
  3.0  3.1  3.2   B   3.4  3.5  3.6   D   3.8  3.9  4.0
```

14. A _____   15. B _____   16. C _____   17. D _____   18. E _____

Connecting Fractions to Decimals

Mixed Applications > STRATEGIES • Write a Number Sentence • Work Backward • Find a Pattern • Draw a Picture

Choose a strategy and solve.

1. Barb gave half of her stamps to Chris. Then she gave 15 stamps to Pat and 9 stamps to Manuel. Barb had 12 stamps left. How many stamps did Barb have at the start?

2. Pablo bought a postcard for $0.35 and a pen that cost 4 times as much as the card. He still had $5.25 left. How much money did he have at the start?

3. A list of numbers starts with 2. Each number is 3 times greater than the number before it. What is the sixth number on the list?

4. Barb spent $36.25 on a collector's stamp and $54.95 on a collector's coin. How much more did the coin cost than the stamp?

5. Carol spent half her money for a coin. Then she spent half of what was left on a stamp. She had $12 left. How much money did Carol have at the start?

6. Yuki has more stamps than Ben. Linda has more stamps than Walter. Linda has 13 fewer stamps than Ben. Who has the most stamps?

MIXED REVIEW

Find the sum or difference. Write each in simplest form.

1. $\frac{1}{5}$ $+\frac{3}{5}$

2. $\frac{3}{6}$ $-\frac{1}{6}$

3. $\frac{1}{8}$ $+\frac{3}{8}$

4. $\frac{7}{9}$ $-\frac{3}{9}$

5. $\frac{5}{10}$ $+\frac{1}{10}$

6. $\frac{9}{12}$ $-\frac{5}{12}$

Equivalent Decimals

Write two equivalent decimals for the shaded part of
each model.

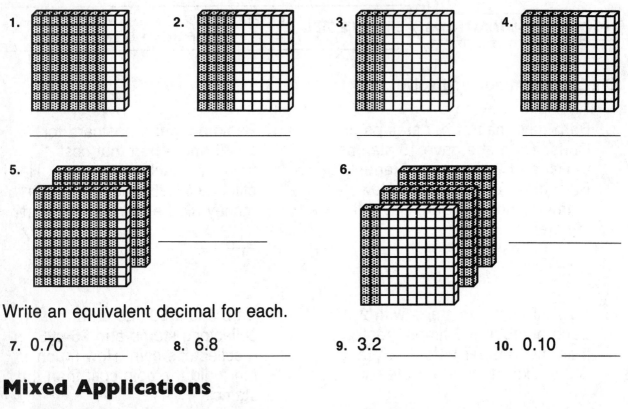

1. _____

2. _____

3. _____

4. _____

5. _____

6. _____

Write an equivalent decimal for each.

7. 0.70 _____

8. 6.8 _____

9. 3.2 _____

10. 0.10 _____

Mixed Applications

11. The Hill Farm has 48.5 acres.
Write an equivalent decimal for
this amount of land.

_____

12. One third of the cows need
shots. There are 36 cows. How
many cows need shots?

_____

EVERYDAY MATH CONNECTION

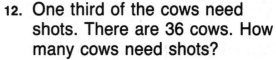

Write a decimal to show what part of 100 pennies each
amount is. (HINT: Decide how many pennies would have
the same value. This number will be the numerator of
a fraction with a denominator of 100. Then write the
fraction as a decimal. For example, 3 dimes = 30
pennies = $\frac{30}{100}$ = 0.30, or 0.3.)

13. 8 dimes _____

14. 5 nickels and 2 pennies _____

15. 3 dimes and 1 nickel _____

16. 1 quarter, 1 dime, and
3 nickels _____

Decimals
Comparing and Ordering

Compare. Write <, >, or = .

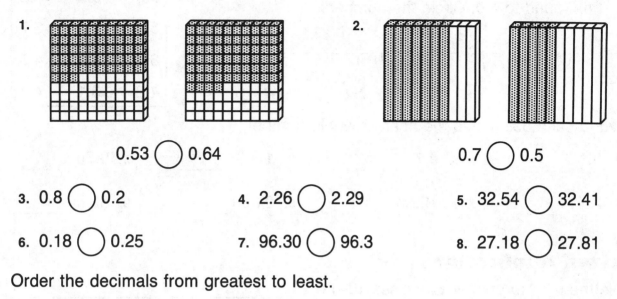

1. 0.53 ◯ 0.64

2. 0.7 ◯ 0.5

3. 0.8 ◯ 0.2

4. 2.26 ◯ 2.29

5. 32.54 ◯ 32.41

6. 0.18 ◯ 0.25

7. 96.30 ◯ 96.3

8. 27.18 ◯ 27.81

Order the decimals from greatest to least.

9. 3.5, 0.46, 5.8, 5.62

10. 52.43, 51.75, 51.7, 52.41

_____

_____

Mixed Applications

Use the table for Exercises 11–12.

Kent School Throwing Contest

Student	Throwing Distance (m)
Carmen	18.08
Beatrice	22.95
Christopher	20.5
Joseph	22.36
Irene	18.8

11. Which student threw the softball the greatest distance? the shortest distance?

_____

12. Who threw the softball farther, Christopher or Joseph?

_____

NUMBER SENSE

Use the digits 4, 5, 6, and 7. Use each digit only once.

13. Write the largest decimal number possible. _____ _____ . _____ _____

14. Write the smallest decimal number possible. _____ _____ . _____ _____

Decimals

Estimation and Rounding

1. Use the number line to find which numbers in the box round to 4.0. Circle the numbers.

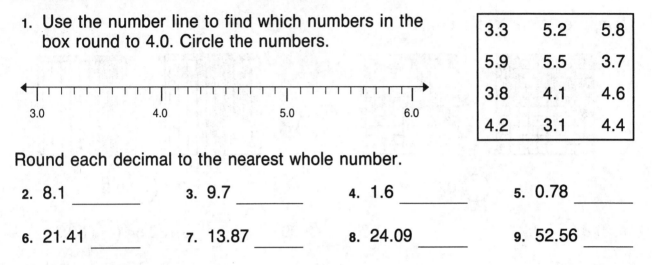

3.3	5.2	5.8
5.9	5.5	3.7
3.8	4.1	4.6
4.2	3.1	4.4

Round each decimal to the nearest whole number.

2. 8.1 _____

3. 9.7 _____

4. 1.6 _____

5. 0.78 _____

6. 21.41 _____

7. 13.87 _____

8. 24.09 _____

9. 52.56 _____

Mixed Applications

Use the map to answer Exercises 10–11.

10. What is the shortest distance between Brookby and Ed's Peak?

_____

11. To the nearest kilometer, how far is it from the Naylor Bridge to Taylorville along the Wagman River Trail? Round your answer.

_____

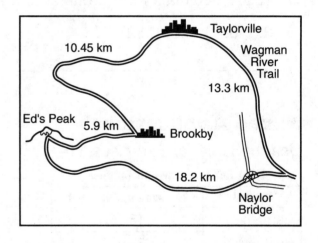

LANGUAGE ARTS CONNECTION

Newspaper headlines use both exact numbers and rounded numbers. Read each headline below. Tell if the number is *exact* or *rounded*.

12. Taxes Cut by $200,000

_____

13. Hospital Fire—42 Injured

_____

14. STB Sells Airline for $3.2 Billion

_____

15. Dow Jones up 9.46 Points

_____

Estimating Sums and Differences

Estimate the sum or difference by using front-end digits.

1.	2.	3.	4.	5.
4.68	9.24	16.24	8.56	8.30
+ 3.25	− 7.38	+ 3.89	− 4.92	+ 16.58

Estimate by rounding to the nearest whole number.

6. $8.74 + 3.64$ _____

7. $12.09 - 3.86$ _____

8. $60.42 - 19.75$ _____

9. $29.79 + 19.89 + 1.98$ _____

10. $2.10 + 3.98 + 23.75$ _____

Mixed Applications

11. The two sections of the Pennant Park bike trail measure 9.65 km and 7.8 km. Estimate the total length of the trail by rounding the length of each section to the nearest whole number.

_____

12. Donya rode the first section of the bike trail in 21.7 minutes. Chong rode the trail in 25.2 minutes. About how much faster was Donya's time? Estimate by rounding.

_____

EVERYDAY MATH CONNECTION

Round the amount on the grocery receipt to the nearest dollar to estimate the total. Then answer the question.

13. You have $25.

```
Store # 104B
Customer Receipt

 $ 5.20
 $ 6.98
 $ 3.88
 $ 7.59
```

Estimate _____

Do you have enough money? _____

14. You have $14.

```
Store # 104B
Customer Receipt

 $ 3.25
 $ 4.99
 $ 7.14
 $ 0.98
```

Estimate _____

About how much more money will you need? _____

Exploring
Adding and Subtracting Decimals

Find the sum and difference for each pair of pictures.

1.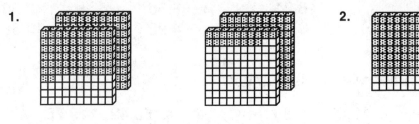

_____   _____

Show each problem on the place-value chart. Solve.

3. 4.6 + 3.84 + 15.07 = n.

Tens	Ones	Tenths	Hundredths
___	___	___	___

4. 36.8 + 4.06 + 14.75 = n

Tens	Ones	Tenths	Hundredths
___	___	___	___

5. 9.1 − 3.7 = n

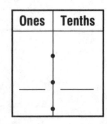

Ones	Tenths
___	___

6. 4.2 − 1.8 = n

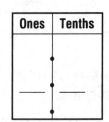

Ones	Tenths
___	___

7. 18.62 − 12.8 = n

Tens	Ones	Tenths	Hundredths
___	___	___	___

MIXED REVIEW

Write the equivalent measure.

1. 16 pints = _____ quarts

2. 15 cups = _____ pints _____ cup

3. 4 gallons = _____ cups

4. 11 pints = _____ gallon _____ pints

Use a customary ruler to measure each line segment.

5. ▬▬▬▬▬▬▬▬▬▬   _____

6. ▬▬▬▬▬▬▬▬▬▬▬▬▬   _____

Problem-Solving Strategy
Use Estimation

Use estimation to solve.

1. Shelly and her father attended a family reunion. The train tickets cost $19.80 each, lunch cost a total of $12.25, and their share of the reunion dinner cost $39.50. About how much were their total expenses?

   _____

2. Aunt Beth traveled 9.8 kilometers from her home to Uncle Budd's. From Uncle Budd's they traveled 24.6 kilometers to the restaurant where the reunion was held. About how far did Aunt Beth travel to get to the reunion?

   _____

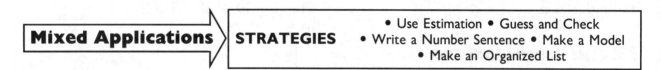

Mixed Applications > **STRATEGIES** • Use Estimation • Guess and Check • Write a Number Sentence • Make a Model • Make an Organized List

Choose a strategy and solve.

3. Uncle Tim ordered the reunion dinner. There was a choice of chicken or beef. The vegetable choices were carrots, peas, or green beans. How many different meat and vegetable combinations were there?

   _____

4. Rosa put flowers on the tables. She put three flowers in each of the red vases, and four flowers in each of the white vases. She used 37 flowers. How many red vases and how many white vases did she use?

   _____

   _____

WRITER'S CORNER

5. Create a plan for your own family reunion. About how many people would you invite? Tell how you would organize the reunion, what activities you would have, and how you would contact everyone.

   _____

   _____

   _____

   _____

Adding Decimals

Find the sum. You may use a calculator.

1. 0.74
    +0.08

2. 19.6
    + 4.7

3. 4.56
    +0.96

4. 0.75
    +8.57

5. 42.8
    + 9.7

6. 4.32
    +2.49

7. 42.08
    + 16.43

8. 23.82
    + 18.56

9. 2.95
    14.86
    + 9.09

10. 7.68
     9.50
     +8.94

11. 0.42 + 1.87 + 9 = n _____

12. 2.67 + 5 + 0.38 = n _____

13. 7.6 + 4.8 + 12 = n _____

14. 18.09 + 32.45 + 6 = n _____

Mixed Applications

15. The butcher receives a shipment of 57.3 kilograms of beef and 42.75 kilograms of chicken. What is the total amount of the shipment?

    _____

16. A package of turkey slices sells for $4.68 each or 2 packages for $9.04. Which is the better buy?

    _____

LOGICAL REASONING

Look at the mixed number. Cross out the decimals in each row that are not equivalent to the mixed number. There may be more than one equivalent number in each row. (HINT: Write an equivalent mixed number that has a fraction using tenths or hundredths. Then write the decimal. For example, $1\frac{1}{5} = 1\frac{2}{10} = 1.2 = 1.20$.)

17. $7\frac{1}{2}$

| 7.05 | 7.5 | 7.50 | 7.55 |

18. $9\frac{2}{5}$

| 90.4 | 9.4 | 9.04 | 9.2 |

19. $6\frac{3}{50}$

| 6.3 | 6.06 | 6.6 | 60.6 |

Subtracting Decimals

Find the difference.

1. 7.8
   − 2.5

2. 5.63
   − 2.32

3. 5.46
   − 3.08

4. 9.40
   − 5.76

5. 8.36
   − 2.97

6. 25.00
   − 8.93

7. 42.06
   − 3.95

8. 72.45
   − 34.68

9. 5.49
   − 3.58

10. 16.09
    − 7.58

11. $8.6 - 4.74 = n$ _____

12. $9.3 - 2.8 = n$ _____

13. $9 - 3.16 = n$ _____

14. $35 - 12.91 = n$ _____

Mixed Applications

Use the table to answer Exercises 15–18.

15. How many seconds longer did it take Tom to run the 200 meters than the 100 meters?

_____

16. How long did it take Bianca to run both races?

_____

17. In the 200-meter race, how many seconds faster is Suki's time than Joshua's?

_____

Erie School Junior Olympics Running Times (in seconds)

	100 meters	200 meters
Bianca	21.52	42.3
Tom	20.85	43.8
Suki	22.84	44.6
Joshua	23.4	46
Derrick	24	45.87

18. What is Derrick's combined time for both races?

_____

WRITER'S CORNER

19. Write an addition problem and a subtraction problem using the decimals 8.2 and 2.65.

_____

_____

Exploring
Dividing by Multiples of Ten

Write the basic fact that helps you find each quotient. Solve.

1. 30)‾120‾ fact: _____

2. 20)‾160‾ fact: _____

3. 40)‾280‾ fact: _____

4. 50)‾300‾ fact: _____

On graph paper, draw a model for each problem.
Solve.

5. $100 \div 20 = n$ _____

6. $120 \div 60 = n$ _____

Record each quotient in the place-value chart.

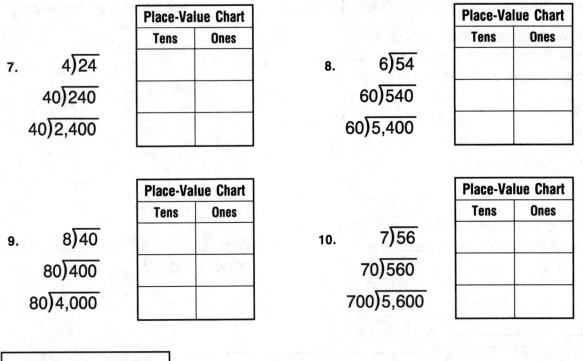

7. 4)‾24‾
   40)‾240‾
   40)‾2,400‾

Place-Value Chart	
Tens	**Ones**

8. 6)‾54‾
   60)‾540‾
   60)‾5,400‾

Place-Value Chart	
Tens	**Ones**

9. 8)‾40‾
   80)‾400‾
   80)‾4,000‾

Place-Value Chart	
Tens	**Ones**

10. 7)‾56‾
    70)‾560‾
   700)‾5,600‾

Place-Value Chart	
Tens	**Ones**

NUMBER SENSE

Write <, >, or = to compare the quotients.

11. $56 \div 8$ ◯ $560 \div 80$

12. $15 \div 3$ ◯ $1,500 \div 30$

13. $280 \div 70$ ◯ $28 \div 7$

14. $3,600 \div 60$ ◯ $360 \div 60$

Estimating Quotients

Complete. Use compatible numbers to estimate.

1. $179 \div 31 = n$

   _____ $\div 30 = 6$

2. $483 \div 59 = n$

   $480 \div$ _____ $= 8$

3. $195 \div 38 = n$

   $200 \div$ _____ $=$ _____

4. $209 \div 67 = n$

   $210 \div$ _____ $=$ _____

5. $321 \div 42 = n$

   _____ $\div 40 =$ _____

6. $397 \div 51 = n$

   _____ $\div 50 =$ _____

Estimate the quotient.

7. $42\overline{)82}$

8. $19\overline{)173}$

9. $71\overline{)495}$

10. $48\overline{)157}$

11. $38\overline{)321}$

12. $21\overline{)105}$

13. $89\overline{)185}$

14. $42\overline{)308}$

15. $62\overline{)375}$

16. $83\overline{)650}$

Mixed Applications

17. Mr. Blume rents an average of 250 video games each week. His store is open 6 days a week. About how many video games does Mr. Blume rent per day?

   _____

18. Mr. Blume arranges his videotapes on shelves. Each shelf holds 32 tapes. He places 241 comedy tapes on shelves. How many shelves hold comedy tapes?

   _____

LOGICAL REASONING

19. A video store is moving to a new location. The stock of 176 videotapes can be packed into cartons that hold 18, 20, and 22 tapes. Which size would be best suited to the mover's needs? Explain your answer. You may use a calculator.

   _____

   _____

   _____

Problem Solving
Find the Hidden Question

Find the hidden question. Solve.

1. George works 4 hours a day at Sound Station. He can unpack a carton in 20 minutes. George has 3 cartons to unpack today. How much time does George have to do other work?

2. George orders cassette tapes from recording companies. This week he has placed orders totaling $98 and $47. How much money is left in his weekly budget of $250?

3. George records two 16-minute programs and one 27-minute program on a 2-hour tape cassette. How much time is left on the tape?

4. A tape recorder cost $500. Mrs. Gray has saved $256. She adds $78 from her paycheck. How much more does she need to buy the tape recorder?

Mixed Applications > **STRATEGIES** • Find the Hidden Question • Work Backward • Guess and Check • Draw a Picture

Choose a strategy and solve.

5. Cassette tapes come in packages of 12 or 16. George orders 5 packages and gets a total of 76 tapes. How many 12-packs and how many 16-packs does George order?

6. Paula buys two 90-minute tapes for $2.49 each and one 60-minute tape. Her total bill is $6.97. How much does a 60-minute tape cost?

MIXED REVIEW

Estimate the product or quotient.

1. $63 \times 13 =$ _____   2. $21 \times 12 =$ _____   3. $59 \times 22 =$ _____   4. $88 \times 41 =$ _____

5. $4\overline{)3,175}$ 6. $6\overline{)5,500}$ 7. $8\overline{)4,725}$ 8. $7\overline{)5,000}$ 9. $9\overline{)7,327}$

146

Dividing by Tens with Remainders

Draw ■ where the first digit in the quotient should be placed.

1. 60)365
2. 40)250
3. 70)295
4. 90)189
5. 50)475

Find the quotient. Check by multiplying.

6. 30)68 Check
7. 20)88 Check
8. 60)331 Check

9. 50)268 Check
10. 40)295 Check
11. 80)500 Check

Mixed Applications

12. A radio station gave sun visors to 270 people on Fun Day. There were 30 visors in each carton. How many cartons of visors did the station give away?

_____

13. The station sells 140 tickets for a raffle to the public. Each raffle ticket sells for 50 cents. How much does the station collect from raffle ticket sales?

_____

SOCIAL STUDIES CONNECTION

14. By 1991, the cost of mailing a letter had changed nine times since the 1850's. The cost for a sheet of 50 stamps is given for several years. Find the cost of one stamp. (HINT: $1.00 = 100 pennies)

1863	1885	1963	1974	1981	1988	1991
$3.00	$1.00	$2.50	$5.00	$10.00	$12.50	$14.50

_____ _____ _____ _____ _____ _____ _____

147

Exploring
Dividing with Two-Digit Divisors

Find each quotient. Use place-value blocks to help you.

1. 12$\overline{)49}$

2. 24$\overline{)98}$

3. 31$\overline{)94}$

4. 20$\overline{)67}$

5. 21$\overline{)108}$

6. 42$\overline{)169}$

7. 90$\overline{)237}$

8. 85$\overline{)425}$

9. 72$\overline{)377}$

10. 63$\overline{)260}$

11. 19$\overline{)143}$

12. 47$\overline{)255}$

13. 32$\overline{)224}$

14. 52$\overline{)321}$

15. 29$\overline{)281}$

16. 38$\overline{)230}$

| WRITER'S CORNER |

17. Write the steps for dividing 699 by 86. Write as if you
were thinking aloud, so that it would be easy for someone
else to follow the steps and understand your solution.

_____

_____

_____

More Two-Digit Divisors

Find the quotient.

1. $53\overline{)106}$ 2. $44\overline{)243}$ 3. $64\overline{)320}$ 4. $32\overline{)224}$

5. $35\overline{)142}$ 6. $23\overline{)115}$ 7. $77\overline{)539}$ 8. $93\overline{)651}$

9. $42\overline{)252}$ 10. $85\overline{)686}$ 11. $65\overline{)391}$ 12. $29\overline{)116}$

13. $74\overline{)592}$ 14. $21\overline{)126}$ 15. $91\overline{)646}$ 16. $82\overline{)332}$

Mixed Applications

17. The space museum is visited by 424 visitors each day. How many people visit the space museum in a two-week period?

_____

18. On Monday, 138 students used the subway to get to the space museum. Each subway car holds 46 people. How many subway cars were used by students on Monday?

_____

LOGICAL REASONING

19. Find six pairs of numbers that could be substituted for n and x in the sentence $n \div x = 50$.

$n =$ _____ , $x =$ _____ $n =$ _____ , $x =$ _____ $n =$ _____ , $x =$ _____

$n =$ _____ , $x =$ _____ $n =$ _____ , $x =$ _____ $n =$ _____ , $x =$ _____

Problem Solving
Interpret the Remainder

Interpret the quotient and the remainder.

1. Mr. Topaz is planting tomato plants. He wants to put exactly 15 plants in each row. He has 137 plants. How many full rows can he plant?

2. Marian has 106 photographs to put in a new album. Each page holds 16 photographs. How many photographs will there be on the last page?

3. Ms. Plummer needs to cover 235 square feet of land with gravel. Each bag of gravel will cover 32 square feet. How many bags of gravel will Ms. Plummer need?

4. Jennifer wants to buy a camera that costs $123. She saves $8 per week. In how many weeks will Jennifer have enough to buy the camera?

| Mixed Applications | STRATEGIES | • Use Estimation • Draw a Picture • Guess and Check • Write a Number Sentence |

Choose a strategy and solve.

5. A Meal Deal at Mardy's costs $2.49. Is $10.00 enough to buy 5 Meal Deals?

6. Penny spends $5.20 on bus fare for 4 round-trips. What is the cost of a one-way bus fare?

VISUAL THINKING

Interpret the quotient and the remainder.

7.

How many bunches?

8.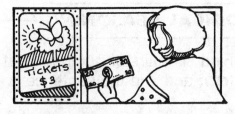

How many tickets?

Two-Digit Quotients

Draw ■ where the first digit in the quotient should be placed.

1. $43\overline{)567}$ 2. $29\overline{)304}$ 3. $17\overline{)249}$ 4. $63\overline{)495}$ 5. $23\overline{)96}$

Estimate by using compatible numbers. Find the
quotient by using repeated subtraction. Use a calculator.

6. Estimate ___   7. Estimate ___   8. Estimate ___   9. Estimate ___

   $43\overline{)97}$ $67\overline{)250}$ $32\overline{)135}$ $83\overline{)175}$

Find the quotient.

10. $28\overline{)793}$ 11. $36\overline{)582}$ 12. $70\overline{)856}$ 13. $42\overline{)652}$

Mixed Applications

Complete the table. Then use it for Exercise 14.

Rico's Photo Shop: Film Purchased in 1993		
Film Type	Amount per wk.	Amount per yr.
110-12	25 rolls	
135-24	63 rolls	
135-36		988 rolls

14. How many rolls of 110 and 135 film were purchased during the year?

_____

WRITER'S CORNER

15. Explain how you decide where the first digit in a quotient should be placed.

_____

_____

Dividing Money

Find the quotient. You may use a calculator.

1. $17\overline{)\$612}$ 2. $34\overline{)\$204}$ 3. $14\overline{)\$322}$ 4. $39\overline{)\$468}$ 5. $23\overline{)\$644}$

6. $13\overline{)\$377}$ 7. $59\overline{)\$826}$ 8. $33\overline{)\$297}$ 9. $17\overline{)\$476}$ 10. $21\overline{)\$483}$

Mixed Applications

11. In the first hour of the Film Festival, the Old-Time Snapshot Company collected $460. At $20 per snapshot, how many snapshots were taken?

_____

12. If the Old-Time Snapshot Company continues to earn $460 per hour, how much money can they hope to collect during the 6-hour Film Festival?

_____

13. The Old-Time Snapshot Company paid $2,120 in salaries to 3 photographers. They paid $53 for each 5-hour shift the photographers worked. Complete the table to show the hours each photographer worked.

Old-Time Snapshot Company

Name	Shifts Worked	Pay
Hans		$689
Frans		$477
Marika		$954

14. What is the total number of hours worked?

_____

EVERYDAY MATH CONNECTION

15. Find the price per pound for each item.

turkey 11 lb. $22   ground beef 15 lb. $45   prime rib roast 12 lb. $132   Salmon 9 lb. $63

_____   _____   _____   _____

Core Skills: Math, Grade 4, Answer Key

Page 1
1. 3, 0
2. 0, 4
3. 8, 0
4. 4, 0
5. false
6. false
7. true
8. true
9. true
10. false
11. 100
12. 500
13. 1,000

Page 2
1. 60
2. 40
3. 9
4. 80
5. 70
6. 320
7. 3 thousands 8 hundreds; 38 hundreds; 380 tens; 3,800 ones
8. 1 thousand 4 hundreds; 14 hundreds; 140 tens; 1,400 ones
9. 4 thousands 5 hundreds; 45 hundreds; 450 tens; 4,500 ones
10. 6 thousands 3 hundreds; 63 hundreds; 630 tens; 6,300 ones
11. 3 thousands 7 hundreds; 37 hundreds; 370 tens; 3,700 ones
12. 5,300; 5,400; 5,500; 5,600; 5,700
13. 2,860; 2,960; 3,060; 3,160; 3,260
14. 9,034; 9,134; 9,234; 9,334; 9,434

Page 3
1. 10,607; ten thousand, six hundred seven
2. 90,500; 90,000 + 500
3. 30,000 + 4,000 + 60 + 9; thirty-four thousand, sixty-nine
4. 7,864; seven thousand, eight hundred sixty-four
5. 4,673; 4,000 + 600 + 70 + 3
6. 20,000 + 400 + 80 + 3; twenty thousand, four hundred eighty-three
7. two thousand, three hundred forty-eight

8. 3,915
9. 702 tens; longs
10. 111 hundreds; flats
11. 21 tens 21 ones; longs and units
12. 12 thousands 12 tens 12 ones; cube, longs, and units

Page 4
1. fiction
2. poetry
3. 8 biographies
4. 4 historical fiction books
5. 7 adventure stories
6. Mystery and detective, and science fiction
7. Descriptions will vary.

Page 5
1. 400; 4 hundreds
2. 40,000; 4 ten thousands
3. 40; 4 tens
4. 400,000; 4 hundred thousands
5. 30,000; 3 ten thousands
6. 0 tens
7. 8,000; 8 thousands
8. 900,000; 9 hundred thousands
9. 814,206; 800,000 + 10,000 + 4,000 + 200 + 6
10. 4 zeros; 40,000
11. 289,300; 200,000 + 80,000 + 9,000 + 300
12. a. subtract 40,000
    b. add 20

Page 6
1. thousands
2. millions
3. ones
4. 68,016,018
5. 640,540,086
6. 13,579,410
7. 835,270,100
8. false
9. true
10. false
11. true
12. a. 8
    b. 1

Page 7
1. >
2. <
3. >
4. <
5. >

6. <
7. 52 < 56
8. 67 < 76
9. 1,239 < 1,339
10. 84 > 48
11. 2,094 > 2,049
12. 26,847 > 26,784
13. 2,875 m
14. 924 m
15. Mount McKinley
16. Mount Rushmore
17. Mount Rainier

Page 8
1. 487 < 493 < 495; 486, 487, 488, 489, 490, 491, 492, 493, 494
2. 350 < 500 < 650 < 850; 200, 300, 400, 500, 600, 700, 800, 900
3. 820 < 840 < 880 < 890; 810, 820, 830, 840, 850, 860, 870, 880, 890
4. 763; 785; 812
5. 136; 149; 175
6. 4,364; 4,390; 4,618
7. 929; 959; 990; 995
8. 7,604; 7,640; 7,642; 7,697
9. Mesa Verde National Park
10. Zion; Mesa Verde; Acadia
11. 9
12. 0
13. 0

Page 9
1–4. Check drawings.
5. add 100
6. 98
7. Clara, June, Pat
8. 1, 1, 1, 1, 1, 2, 2, 1, 1, 1, 1, 1, 2, 2
Mixed Review
1. 800 + 50 + 6
2. 4,000 + 300 + 10 + 5
3. 90,000 + 500 + 7
4. 66,702
5. 184,913
6. 2,407,854

Page 10
1. twenty-third
2. eighty-eighth
3. thirty-first
4. fifty-seventh
5. ninety-sixth
6. sixty-fifth
7. 37th, 40th
8. 30th, 40th, 50th
9. 89th, 90th

Core Skills: Math, Grade 4, Answer Key (cont.)

Page 10 (cont.)
10. 75th, 79th
11. 8
12. 9, 15, 18
13. eighth
14. Wednesday
15. Thursday
16. November 4
17. fourth place
18. 7 people
19. 3rd place

Page 11
1. 50
2. $3.80
3. 70
4. $1.50
5. 90
6. $1.30
7. 560
8. 230
9. 500
10. 200
11. $8.00
12. 200
13. 7,000
14. 2,000
15. 3,000
16. 1,000
17. 4,200 mi
18. 375 mi; 384 mi
19. 496 mi
20. 2,194 mi
21. 1,459 mi

Page 12
1. 7; Zero
2. 18; Doubles
3. 15; Doubles Plus One
4. 7; Counting On
5. 6; Doubles
6. 7; Counting On, Doubles Plus One
7. 9; Zero
8. 11; Doubles Plus One
9. 5
10. 10
11. 17
12. 11
13. 6
14. 11
15. 13
16. 16
17. 11
18. 6
19. 7
20. 6
21. 9 cards

22. 11 hr
23. 8, 10, 11; 17, 16, 15, 11
24. Add 2; 8, 9; Add 9; 8, 9

Page 13
1–6. Groupings may vary. One possible grouping is given.
1. 12; (3 + 5) + 4 = 12
2. 17; 2 + (7 + 8) = 17
3. 13; (4 + 1) + 8 = 13
4. 15; 4 + (5 + 6) = 15
5. 18; (9 + 2) + 7 = 18
6. 14; 7 + (3 + 4) = 14
7. 12
8. 16
9. 16
10. 17
11. 14
12. 13
13. 14
14. 16
15. 18
16. 13
17. 16
18. 16
19. 11
20. 18
21. 13
22. 16
23. 12, 14, 12
24. November
25. Answers will vary.

Page 14
1. $7.00
2. 700
3. $8.00
4. $8.00
5. 600
6. 7,000
7–11. Estimates and strategies may vary. Front-end and rounding estimates are given.
7. $10.00–$11.00
8. 900; same
9. $11.00–$12.00
10. 800–900
11. 6,000–8,000
12. about 110 magazines
13. about 130 newspapers
14–17. Estimates may vary.
14. about $4.00
15. about $4.00
16. about $10.00
17. about $9.00

Page 15
1. Sally
2. 38 mi
3. about 50 shawls
4. 15 creatures
5. Maps will vary.
6. 5 km

Page 16
1. 59
2. Ring second column; 81
3. Ring second column; 65
4. Ring second column; 96
5. Ring both columns; 150
6. Ring both columns; 146
7. Ring first column; 128
8. Ring second column; 54
9. Ring second column; 78
10. Ring both columns; 174
11. Ring second column; 60
12. Ring first column; 175
13. Ring both columns; 140
14. 54
15. 98
16. Ring first column; 129
17. Ring both columns; 146
18. 57
19. 163
20. 135
21. 135
22. 133
23. 116
24. 125
25. 143
26. 178
27. 146
28. 161
29. Blue team
30. White team
31. 7, 4
32. 8, 9
33. 4, 1, 5

Page 17
1. Ring last column; 584
2. Ring middle column; 935
3. Ring first and last columns; 1,281
4. Ring first and last columns; 1,280
5. 386
6. Ring first and middle columns; 1,259
7. Ring middle column; 847
8. Ring first and middle columns; 1,125
9. Ring first and middle columns; 1,589

Core Skills: Math, Grade 4, Answer Key (cont.)

Page 17 (cont.)
10. 957
11. 797
12. Ring last column; 881
13. Ring first and middle columns; 1,246
14. Ring all columns; 1,043
15. Ring middle column; 618
16. Ring last column; $4.73
17. Ring middle and last columns; $6.11
18. $3.84
19. Ring first and middle columns; $14.55
20. Ring first column; $11.77
21. $1,125
22. 661 pieces
Mixed Review
1. 60
2. 80
3. 80
4. 40
5. $1.30
6. $0.60
7. $1.50
8. $0.20
9. 600
10. 400
11. 600
12. 900
13. $5.00
14. $6.00
15. $8.00
16. $8.00

Page 18
1. 89
2. 135
3. 1,930
4. 10,305
5. 2,806
6. 126
7. 757
8. $11.20
9. $57.58
10. $7.90
11. 133 min
12. $7.63
13. 5,239 cars; 5,295 cars; 11,266 cars
14–15. More than one arrangement is possible but sum should be as shown with these arrangements.
14. 125 + 249 = 374
15. 942 + 521 = 1,463

Page 19
1. 600
2. 400
3. 400
4. 300
5. 300
6. 3,000
7. 4,000
8. 2,000
9. $10.00
10. $20.00
11. 200
12. 500
13. $60.00
14. 4,000
15. about 400 kinds
16. more than 200
17. 137
18. 1,570

Page 20
1. 54
2. Ring both columns; 37
3. 11
4. Ring both columns; 17
5. Ring both columns; 4
6. 31
7. Ring both columns; 51
8. Ring both columns; 49
9. Ring both columns; 39
10. 10
11. 42
12. Ring both columns; 35
13. Ring both columns; 2
14. 24
15. Ring both columns; 45
16. Ring both columns; 19
17. 32
18. 20
19. 8
20. 18
21. 26
22. 8
23. 56
24. 25
25. 13
26. 19
27. 51
28. 67 garden hoses
29. 46 shovels
30. 8 + 9 = 17; 17 − 8 = 9
31. 9 + 2 = 11; 11 − 9 = 2
32. 3 + 8 = 11; 8 + 3 = 11
33. 11 − 6 = 5; 11 − 5 = 6

Page 21
1. 225
2. 495
3. 604
4. 119

5. 391
6. $6.80
7. $4.08
8. $5.68
9. $5.54
10. $0.59
11. 549
12. 824
13. $0.76
14. $2.94
15. 139 kg
16. 1,433 kg
17. b

Page 22
1. classes offered, days of classes, times classes are given
2. gymnastics or ceramics
3. The times of the classes overlap.
4. 30 students
5. 23 km
6. Answers and tables will vary.

Page 23
1–3. Check work.
1. $5.55
2. $18.67
3. $14.79
4. c; $3.15
5. b; $40.21
6. yes
7. yes

Page 24
1–14. Estimates will vary.
1. [3,000]; 3,186
2. [8,000]; 7,650
3. [4,000]; 3,864
4. [8,000]; 8,052
5. [2,000]; 2,426
6. [5,000]; 4,724
7. [6,000]; 5,369
8. [3,000]; 3,159
9. [11,000]; 11,207
10. [10,000]; 9,650
11. [2,000]; 1,315
12. [1,000]; 1,081
13. [12,000]; 12,206
14. [10,000]; 12,568
15. 319; 2,851; 2,902; 1,133
16. 7,205 kilowatt-hours
Mixed Review
1. >
2. <
3. =
4. 161
5. 584

Core Skills: Math, Grade 4, Answer Key (cont.)

Page 25
1. 3 x 5 = 15
2. 4 x 6 = 24
3. 4 x 3 = 12
4. 12 ÷ 4 = 3 or 12 ÷ 3 = 4
5. 20 ÷ 5 = 4 or 20 ÷ 4 = 5
6. 18 ÷ 6 = 3 or 18 ÷ 3 = 6
7. 6 x 8 = 48; 48 ÷ 6 = 8;
   48 ÷ 8 = 6
8. 32 ÷ 8 = 4; 8 x 4 = 32;
   4 x 8 = 32
9. 7 x 5 = 35; 35 ÷ 7 = 5;
   35 ÷ 5 = 7
10. 3 x 5¢ = 15¢
11. 5 x 5¢ = 25¢
12. 7 x 5¢ = 35¢

Page 26
1–3. Check arrays.
1. 12
2. 24
3. 14
4. 2
5. 8
6. 3
7. 16
8. 18
9. 24
10. 18
11. 10
12. 12
13. 27
14. 14
15. 4
16. 12
17. 6
18. 15
19. 6
20. 21
21. 9
22. 24
23. 15
24. 12
25. 18
26. 8
27. 21
28. 3
29. 16
30. 10 stamps
31. $3.40
32. 27 points
33. 27 points
34. 30 points

Page 27
1–3. Check arrays.
4. 15
5. 25

6. 4
7. 10
8. 24
9. 30
10. 12
11. 35
12. 32
13. 16
14. 20
15. 28
16. 45
17. 8
18. 5
19. 20
20. 40
21. 36
22. 40
23. 15
24. 35
25. 45
26. 20
27. 28
28. 16
29. 32
30. 30 people
31. 12 helicopters
32. <
33. >
34. =
35. >
36. =
37. <

Page 28
1. b
2. c
3. d
4. a
5. a
6. d
7. 35
8. 36
9. 18
10. 16
11. 0
12. 0
13. 4
14. 24
15. 18
16. 0
17. a. 4 x 0 = 0
    b. 4 x 1 = 4
18. a. and c.

Page 29
1. number of children is missing
2. cost of $24.95 is not needed; $1.05

3. blue
4. Jay
5. Answers will vary. Possible answer: 3 of 4 fields planted with trees or shrubs
6. Answers will vary.

Page 30
1–3. Check arrays.
1. 42
2. 28
3. 54
4. 42
5. 6
6. 7
7. 42
8. 14
9. 28
10. 18
11. 49
12. 36
13. 48
14. 56
15. 54
16. 14
17. 36
18. 21
19. 54
20. 30
21. 28 strings
22. 5 pianos
23. Check multiplication wheel.

Page 31
1–3. Check arrays.
1. 32
2. 27
3. 64
4. 72
5. 24
6. 9
7. 56
8. 18
9. 8
10. 63
11. 32
12. 72
13. 64
14. 54
15. 16
16. 45
17. 48
18. 81
19. 27
20. 36
21. 40
22. 56 batches
23. 48 muffins
24. b; 14

Core Skills: Math, Grade 4, Answer Key (cont.)

Page 32
1. 24
2. 54
3. 32
4. 18
5. 56
6. 20
7. 0
8. 16
9. 72
10. 24
11. 35
12. 81
13. 28
14. 30
15. 63
16. 16
17. 0
18. 42
19. 64
20. 21
21. 48
22. 49
23. 6
24. 36
25. 0
26. 45
27. 24, 32, 40, 48, 56, 64, 72
28. 21, 28, 35, 42, 49, 56, 63
29. 64 ears of corn
30. 29 green peppers
Mixed Review
1. $71.14
2. $36.18
3. $44.81
4. $59.09
5. $16.66

Page 33
1. 3 x 4 = 12; 12 ÷ 3 = 4
   or 12 ÷ 4 = 3
2. 3 x 6 = 18; 18 ÷ 6 = 3
   or 18 ÷ 3 = 6
3. 9; 4 x 9 = 36 or 9 x 4 = 36
4. 7; 35 ÷ 5 = 7 or 35 ÷ 7 = 5
5. 8; 72 ÷ 9 = 8 or 72 ÷ 8 = 9
6. 5
7. 9
8. 7
9. b; 9 pots
10. 32
11. 72
12. 36

Page 34
1–3. Check drawings.
1. 3
2. 6
3. 9

4. 9
5. 1
6. 6
7. 2
8. 4
9. 7
10. 7
11. 5
12. 8
13. 2
14. 9
15. 8
16. 2
17. 5
18. 8
19. 3
20. 5
21. 6
22. 4
23. 1
24. 8 cages
25. 8 days
26–28. Check drawings.

Page 35
1–3. Check drawings.
1. 5
2. 5
3. 5
4. 8
5. 7
6. 3
7. 8
8. 7
9. 4
10. 9
11. 1
12. 5
13. 5
14. 3
15. 6
16. 9
17. 2
18. 5 bookshelves
19. $3.15
20. 5, 9
21. 3, 9
22. 8

Page 36
1. 72 ÷ 9 = 8; 8 cages
2. 7 x 2 = 14; 14 bags
3. Bert
4. 45 min
5. 4 x 3 = 12
6. 4 x 2 = 8
7. 4 x 4 = 16
8. 4 x 8 = 32

Page 37
1. 0
2. 1
3. 1
4. 0
5. 18
6. 1
7. 64
8. 7
9. 0
10. 1
11. 17
12. 0
13. 1
14. 0
15. 1
16. 3
17. 1
18. 1
19. 0
20. 1
21. 24
22. 8
23. 0
24. 1
25. 14 hr
26. Ramón
27. $7
28. =
29. <
30. =
31. =

Page 38
1–3. Check drawings.
1. 5
2. 6
3. 3
4. 2
5. 7
6. 3
7. 9
8. 5
9. 9
10. 1
11. 6
12. 4
13. 4
14. 2
15. 7
16. 1
17. 8
18. $45
19. 4 trips
20. how many in each group;
    4 tires
21. how many groups; 8 boxes

Core Skills: Math, Grade 4, Answer Key (cont.)

Page 39
1–3. Check drawings.
1. 4
2. 5
3. 3
4. 7
5. 2
6. 3
7. 7
8. 4
9. 1
10. 5
11. 9
12. 6
13. 8
14. 6
15. 8
16. 1
17. 2
18. 9
19. 3
20. 3
21. 7
22. 2
23. 4
24. 7 roses
25. 54 flowers
Mixed Review
1. 5 x 9 = 45; 45 ÷ 9 = 5;
   45 ÷ 5 = 9
2. 48 ÷ 8 = 6; 6 x 8 = 48;
   8 x 6 = 48
3. 9 x 8 = 72; 72 ÷ 9 = 8;
   72 ÷ 8 = 9

Page 40
1. 7:15; seven-fifteen;
   15 minutes past seven; a
   quarter past seven
2. 4:43; four forty-three; forty-
   three minutes past four;
   seventeen minutes to five
3. 8:30; eight-thirty; thirty
   minutes past eight
4. top clock
5. bottom clock
6. 36 minutes
7. Jason prepared the bread
   dough.
8. b. five-thirty

Page 41
1. 6:30 A.M.
2. 11:00 P.M.
3. 12:15 P.M.
4. Times will vary.
5. Times will vary.

6. whale show
7. 10:45 A.M.
8. 6:00 P.M.
9. 1:00 P.M.

Page 42
1. months
2. minutes
3. minutes
4. second
5. a
6. c
7. about 4:00 (3:55)
8. less than one hour
9. Check clocks.

Page 43
1. 16 hours
2. 65 minutes or 1 hour,
   5 minutes
3. 35 minutes
4. 5 hours
5. 7:45 A.M.
6. 35 minutes
7. 7:10 A.M.
8. 10:15 A.M.; 11:00 A.M.;
   11:45 A.M.; 12:30 P.M.;
   1:15 P.M.

Page 44
1. October 13
2. 9 days
3. October 5
4. Friday, October 25
5. Friday, October 18
6. Monday, October 14
7. $5.21
8. 4/12/93
9. 6/23/94

Page 45
1. Train B
2. Train A
3. one
4. 15 minutes
5. 11:00 A.M.
6. $5.75
7. 3 hours, 36 minutes, 14
   seconds
8. 6 hours, 42 minutes, 5
   seconds

Page 46
1. basketball
2. 15 + 9 = 24 people
3. 42 people
4. Check work.

5. 74 more visitors
6. Game 4
7. Game 5, Game 2, Game 3,
   Game 1, Game 4
8. Frequency tables will vary.

Page 47
1. Wednesday
2. Tuesday
3. 20, 80, 60
4. 80 more boxes of buttons
5. need to know the number of
   buttons in a box
6. 70
7. 50
8. 150

Page 48
1. horizontal
2. the number of students
3. 10 students
4. printmaking
5. clay modeling
6. 165
7. 265 students
Mixed Review
1. 6 x 8 = 48; 48 ÷ 6 = 8;
   48 ÷ 8 = 6
2. 56 ÷ 8 = 7; 8 x 7 = 56;
   7 x 8 = 56
3. 7 x 6 = 42; 42 ÷ 6 = 7;
   42 ÷ 7 = 6

Page 49
1. Check graph.
2. Taylor
3. 31 lawns
4. Bar graphs and sentences
   will vary.

Page 50
1. X
2. R
3. C
4. P
5. U
6. L
7. (8, 3)
8. (0, 4)
9. (8, 10)
10. (6, 6)
11. (2, 8)
12. (7, 9)
13. D, (5, 0); H, (5, 9);
    B, (1, 5); S, (4, 5)
14. Answers will vary.
15. THAT HITS THE SPOT

Core Skills: Math, Grade 4, Answer Key (cont.)

Page 51
1. December
2. July
3. 200, 250, 50
4. August and September
5. July and October
6. September and October
7. 1,150 sales
8. b
9. c

Page 52
1–2. Check graphs.
3. 30 marbles in the blue box and 6 marbles in the red box

Page 53
1–2. Graphs will vary.
3. New Mexico, Arizona, California
4. 200 miles more
5. 2,700 miles
6. more
7. more
8. less

Page 54
1. 6; 60; 600; 6,000
2. 12; 120; 1,200; 12,000
3. 4; 280; 400; 28,000
4. 58 cans
5. 60 cans
6. $4 \times 10 = 40$
7. $4 \times 100 = 400$
8. $4 \times 1,000 = 4,000$

Page 55
1. 160
2. 900
3. 12,000
4. 360
5. 900
6. 24,000
7–11. Estimates may vary. Front-end and rounded estimates are given.
7. 150; 150
8. 360; 420
9. 2,800; 3,500
10. 28,000; 28,000
11. 3,000; 3,000
12. about 200 kilometers
13. about 160 workers
14. about $120
15. 7 hours 45 minutes
16. 67×4
17. 30×9

18. 84×8
19. 6×72

Page 56
1. 27; 90; 600; 717
2. 24; 160; 184
3. 10; 100; 500; 610
4. 72; 80; 152
5. 15; 450; 500; 965
6. $72
7. $3 \times \$22 \times 4 = \$264$
8. Check table.

Page 57
1. 248
2. 201
3. 246
4. 234
5. 837
6. 414
7. 94
8. 180
9. 140 calendars
10. 102 children
11. $17.45
12. 9:45 A.M.
13. 466 calories
14. 567 calories
15. 596 calories

Page 58
1. 574
2. 342
3. 951
4. 875
5. 744
6. 728
7. 770
8. 957
9. 680
10. 984
11. 812
12. 825
13. 880
14. 954
15. 772
16. 868
17. 675 offices
18. 412 offices
19. 642
20. 624
21. 820

Page 59
1–2. Flowcharts may vary.
1. $23
2. 2
3. 90 kilometers

4. Peter
5. ate dinner
Mixed Review
1. 12:30; half-past twelve
2. 7:48; 12 minutes to 8
3. 9:12; nine twelve

Page 60
1. 1,968
2. 1,892
3. 1,953
4. 915
5. 3,625
6. 3,664
7. 2,415
8. 858
9. 8,460
10. 2,970
11. 1,602
12. 1,648
13. 6,944
14. 15 hours
15. $14
16. 468 people
17. 2,108 people
18. 3
19. 3
20. 7, 1, 0

Page 61
1–9. Estimates may vary. Front-end and rounded estimates are given.
1. 4,000; 4,000; 4,192
2. 4,000; 8,000; 7,144
3. 12,000; 12,000; 13,095
4. 28,000; 28,000; 29,032
5. 42,000; 49,000; 45,626
6. 21,000; 28,000; 25,368
7. 24,000; 30,000; 27,798
8. 21,000; 21,000; 21,642
9. 16,000; 24,000; 21,720
10. 23,750 copiers
11. 3,258 newspapers
12. 1 hour 35 minutes
13. 177 customers
14. Answers will vary.

Page 62
Choices of computation methods will vary.
1. 516 cans
2. 60 dogs
3. Sharon
4. $30
5. 24
6. $3 \times 4 \times 3 = 36$ blocks

159

Core Skills: Math, Grade 4, Answer Key (cont.)

Page 63
1. $19.14; $21.00
2. $6.48; $0.80 x 9 = $7.20
3. $27.12; $5.00 x 6 = $30.00
4. $128.55; $50.00 x 3 = $150.00
5. $63.04; $20.00 x 4 = $80.00
6. $21.16; $6.00 x 4 = $24.00
7. $4.10; $0.90 x 5 = $4.50
8. $280.26; $50.00 x 6 = $300.00
9. $78.56; $10.00 x 8 = $80.00
10. $26.46
11. $1.41
12. $11.60
13. $98.55
14. $60.00
15. $29.86
16. $75.50
17. $111.22
18. $110.25

Page 64
1. 80; 800; 8,000
2. 420; 4,200; 42,000
3. 540; 5,400; 54,000
4. 600
5. 800,000
6. 560,000
7. 480,000
8. 18,000,000
9. 4,200 times
10. 2,000 times
11. a. 7,200 times
    b. 1,800 times more
12. =
13. <
14. >
15. =

Page 65
1. 600
2. 800
3. 4,800
4. 600
5. 1,200
6. 5,400
7. $100
8. $540
9. $50
10. $68.00
11. $154.00
12. $77.00
13. about 1,200 houses
14. about $6
15. 3,200
16. 1,250

17. 4,400
18. 3,300

Page 66
1. 5; 90; 900
2. 10; 140; 1,400
3. 1,560
4. 1,150
5. 300
6. 960
7. 2,460
8. 1,440
9. 2,160
10. 3,900
11. 5,360
12. 720 minutes
13. 1,440 minutes
14. 168 hours
15. 240 hours
16. 960 minutes
17. Questions will vary.

Page 67
1. Bar graphs will vary.
2. $26
3. 6 weeks
4. Bar graphs and explanations will vary.

Page 68
1. 54; 120; 540; 1200; 1,914; 174; 1740; 1,914
2. 42; 480; 70; 800; 1,392; 522; 870; 1,392
3. 6; 540; 40; 3600; 4,186; 546; 3640; 4,186
4. 14 x 24 = 336 pages
5. 26 x 19 = 494 newspapers
Mixed Review
1. 300
2. 4,000
3. 32,000
4. 2,800
5. 27,000
6. 7,200
7. 6; 150; 1,500
8. 8; 280; 2,800

Page 69
1. 1,824
2. 3,456
3. 1,428
4. 2,790
5. 1,896
6. 3,648
7. 897
8. 6,750

9. 1,827
10. 2,352
11. $n = 3,120$
12. $n = 2,394$
13. $n = 1,118$
14. $n = 3,128$
15. 2,184 hours
16. 756 miles
17. 384 mi
18. 648 mi
19. 720 mi
20. 616 mi

Page 70
1. 4,140
2. 23,256
3. 8,692
4. 24,928
5. 58,473
6. 45,212
7. 15,996
8. 34,328
9. 1,476 costumes
10. 38 dancers
11. $4,420; $4,680; $5,980; $3,744; $6,240
12. delivery person
13. $1,560 more
14. Answers will vary.

Page 71
1–9. Front-end and rounded estimates are given.
1. [8,000; 9,000]; 9,396
2. [12,000; 15,000]; 15,742
3. [80,000; 120,000]; 119,798
4. [720,000; 720,000]; 750,444
5. [800,000; 1,000,000]; 900,720
6. [28,000; 32,000]; 30,720
7. [100,000; 100,000]; 121,512
8. [24,000; 36,000]; 32,220
9. [700,000; 700,000]; 782,328
10. 10,500
11. 64,875
12. 23,000
13. 2,250 bulbs
14. $9.68
Mixed Review
1. $5.04
2. $14.04
3. $12.36
4. 15,132
5. 72,600

Core Skills: Math, Grade 4, Answer Key (cont.)

Page 72
1. 20 tomato plants; 5 bean plants
2. 4 hours in afternoon; 2 hours after dinner
3. Hilda
4. green
5. $43.95
6. $32
7. 70
8. 8,000
9. 10
10. 7,000
11. 20
12. 800
13. 75
14. 300
15. 7,000

Page 73
1. $223.08
2. $113.16
3. $1,833.72
4. $15.64
5. $1,496.25
6. $331.38
7. $122.16
8. $53.55
9. $537.81
10. $3,514.68
11. $83.40
12. $356.70
13. $2,386.94
14. $468.00
15. $806.25
16. $189.25
17. 1 quarter, 1 dime, 2 nickels, 2 pennies
18. 40 pennies, 2 dimes, 8 nickels

Page 74
1–7. Check measurements.
8. No. 45 + 45 = 90 inches, which is less than the 96 inches Lee needs.
9. Answers will vary, depending on type of unit chosen.
10. Answers will vary.

Page 75
1. 2 cm
2. 6 cm
3. 1 dm
4. cm or dm
5. m
6. km
7. cm

8. 5 dm
9. 10 m
10. 16 km
11. 2 m
12. 49 km
13. Fay (15 stickers)
14. 48 km, 85 km, 133 km

Page 76
1. in.
2. ft
3. yd
4. 3 yd
5. 16 ft
6. 23 mi
7. 400 yd
8. Mel
9. ruler
10. Mississippi
11. 1,040 mi
12. Tennessee
13. in.
14. mi
15. ft

Page 77
1–4. Check drawings.
1. ducks
2. Cheryl
3. green, blue, red, blue, blue, red, blue, blue, red, green
4. Alex
5. $7.01
6. Gordon grew 2 cm more than Maya.
7. Problems will vary.

Page 78
1–4. Answers will vary.
5. 2 + 3 + 3 + 2 + 5 = P; P = 15 cm
6. 4 + 4 + 4 + 4 + 4 + 4 + 4 + 4 = P, or 8 x 4 = P; P = 32 cm
7. 36 in.
8. 52 cm

Mixed Review
1. 7,182
2. 2,240
3. 768
4. 4,402
5. 7,812
6. 3 hours, 25 minutes
7. 14 hours, 10 minutes

Page 79
1. gal
2. c
3. gal

4. qt
5. tbsp
6. C, or pt
7. 2 pints
8. 12 persons
9–10. Answers will vary. Possible answers are given.
9. gallons, gallon, tablespoon
10. pints, quart, cups

Page 80
1. 8 gallons
2. 40 minutes
3. 657 miles
4. 108 inches
5. $31
6. sparkle flashlight: 57¢; plain flashlight: 42¢
7. Check problems.

Page 81
1. L
2. mL
3. L
4. mL
5. 1 mL
6. 500 mL
7. 120 mL
8. c
9. b
10. b
11. the wide vase
12. 2 liters
13. Change 350 L to 350 mL.
14. Change 200mL to 20 mL.
15. Change 2,500 mL to 250 mL.
16. Change 4 mL to 4 L.

Page 82
1. g
2. g
3. kg
4. kg
5. g
6. kg
7. 1 g
8. 1,750 kg
9. 20 g
10. 450 kg
11. 3 kg
12. 725 grams
13. Put the 5 kg and 10 kg weights on one side of the scale, and the 1 kg weight on the other side. Add oranges to the 1 kg side until the scale is balanced.

Core Skills: Math, Grade 4, Answer Key (cont.)

Page 83
1. oz
2. lb
3. lb
4. T
5. lb
6. oz
7. 1 lb
8. 7 lb
9. 5 oz
10. 80
11. 26,000
12. 4
13. pounds
14. 4 lb, 8 oz
15. 3 pounds

Page 84
1. true
2. false
3. false
4. true
5. 24
6. 45
7. 9
8. 8 ounces
9. 16 ounces, or 1 pound, of nuts
10. 3 bracelets
11. no
12. 12, 24, 36, 48, 60
13. 9, 18, 27, 36, 45
14. 8, 16, 24, 32, 40
15. 32, 64, 96, 128, 160

Page 85
1. three
2. four
3. one
4. three
5. three
6. 4, 40, 400
7. 3, 30, 300
8. 8, 80, 800
9. 7, 70, 700
10. 7; 70; 700; 7,000
11. 8; 80; 800; 8,000
12. 9; 90; 900; 9,000
13. 5; 50; 500; 5,000
14. 200 books
15. 50 books

Page 86
1. 7 r2
2. 35, 40, 45; 8 r2
3. 24, 32, 40; 4 r3
4. 4 r3
5. 7 r1

6. 6 r1
7. 3 r4
8. 7
9. 8
10. 62
11. 6
12. 5 full rows; 3 cyclists on the unfilled row
13. 266 passengers
14. 3
15. 63

Page 87
1. 23
2. 13
3. 21
4. 18
5. 14
6. 15
7. 13
8. 11
9. 27
10. 24
11–17. Check answers.

Page 88
1. b; compatible numbers
2. c; compatible numbers
3. a; compatible numbers
4–19. Estimates may vary. One compatible number estimate is given.
4. 50
5. 60
6. 40
7. 30
8. 20
9. 70
10. 80
11. 20
12. 80
13. 80
14. 30
15. 60
16. 60
17. 70
18. 90
19. 70
20. about 80 seats
21. about 60 minutes
Mixed Review
1–5. Estimates may vary.
1. 400
2. 11,000
3. 1,300
4. 70,000
5. 13,000

Page 89
1. 5
2. 0
3. 15
4. 23
5. 45 public stations
6. 28 more stations
7. $22
8. 12 times
9. 3 hours more
10. 6 hours
11. Check problems.

Page 90
1–6. Check problems.
7. 17
8. 13 r3
9. 13 r4
10. 24
11. 21 r3
12. 13
13. 29 r2
14. 11 r5
15. $8.34
16. 14 letters of each color
17. 4

Page 91
1–5. Check problems.
6. 84 r2
7. 65
8. 122 r5
9. 83 r4
10. About 81
11. About 189
12. About 97
13. records
14. 118 tapes on each shelf
15. 2
16. 33
17. 114
18. 62

Page 92
1–5. Check problems. Estimates may vary. One possible estimate is given.
6. 103 r1; Estimate: 100
7. 202 r1; Estimate: 200
8. 107 r3; Estimate: 100
9. 100 r2
10. 100 r1
11. 200 r3
12. about 91 days
13. 199
Mixed Review
1. 5 r2
2. 6 r1

Core Skills: Math, Grade 4, Answer Key (cont.)

Page 92 (cont.)
3. 6 r3
4–8. Estimates may vary. One possible estimate is given.
4. 8
5. 7
6. 5
7. 2
8. 7

Page 93
1. $0.93
2. $1.70
3. $2.04
4. $0.87
5. $0.79
6. $1.20
7. $4.07
8. $0.68
9. $1.15
10. $2.43
11. $0.33 per ounce
12. Answers will vary.

Page 94
1. mental math; 300 issues
2. calculator; $106.25
3. 258 different magazines
4. no
5. on the left end
6. 5:55 A.M.
7. Check problems.

Page 95
1. 5 stacks
2. 9 + 6 + 7 + 10 + 3 = 35
3. 7 cubes
4. 7 photographs
5. 35 ÷ 5 = 7
6. 29 + 58 + 84 = 171;
   171 ÷ 3 = 57; 57 days

Page 96
1. 5, 7, 6
2. 35, 20, 33
3. 6, 7, 7
4. 26, 17, 27
5. 79, 48, 85
6. 102, 30, 109
7. 88
8. 91
9. 11, 19, 12
10. Answers will vary.

Page 97
1. Possible answers: cylinder, cone
2. Possible answers: pyramid

3. Possible answers: pyramid, cube, rectangular prism
4. solid
5. plane
6. plane
7. solid
8. rectangular prism
9. cylinder
10. cone
11. pyramid
12. cone
13. cylinder
14. cube
15. rectangular prism
16. Descriptions will vary.

Page 98
1. true
2. true
3. false
4. no; not closed
5. yes
6. no; all sides not straight
7. yes
8. quadrilateral
9. triangle
10. octagon
11. hexagon
12. octagon; 8
13. triangle; 3

Page 99
1–3. Check drawings.
4. 12 square units
5. 13 square units
6. 25 square units; 5 units x 5 units = 25 square units
7. 18 square units; 6 units x 3 units = 18 square units
8. B and C
9. A and B; C and D
10. 270,000 sq km
11. 178,200 sq km

Page 100
1. 64 miles
2. $7.22
3. $669
4. 348 photos
5. 3:45 P.M.
6. 800 square feet
7. 73 pesos
8. 19 pesos
9. 37 pesos

Page 101
1. line segment
2. ray

3. point
4. line
5–7. Check drawings.
8. no
9. yes
10. no
11. no
12. Perimeter: 4 units;
    Area: 1 square unit
13. 11 markers
14. a star

Page 102
1. acute
2. right
3. obtuse
4. acute
5. right
6. obtuse
7. acute
8. 3 acute angles
9. 2 acute angles
10. 3 acute angles
11. 1 acute angle
Mixed Review
1. 5,489
2. 75,618
3. 121,888
4. 5,872
5. 16,233
6. 60
7. 146 r3
8. 52 r1
9. 73 r3
10. $2.16
11. 23, 15, 22
12. 53, 27, 51

Page 103
1–4. Answers will vary.
     Possible answers are given.
1. parallel lines
2. perpendicular lines
3. intersecting lines
4. ray
5–7. Check drawings.
8. 3:00 and 9:00
9. 1:50
10–12. Answers will vary.
     Accept reasonable
     definitions.

Page 104
1–3. Answers will vary. Check drawings.
4. point *M*
5. radii *MA, MT, MH*
6. diameter *AH*

Page 104 (cont.)
7. diameter
8. point S
9. radius
10. diameter
11. Answers will vary.

Page 105
1. both
2. similar
3. both
4. both
5. both
6. similar
7–8. Check drawings.
9. The social studies map and the wall map are similar. They have the same shape but different sizes. The third map will be similar to the others. All maps of the United States should be similar.

Page 106
1–2. Check drawings.
3. 16 and 48
4. 54 hexagons
Mixed Review
1. rectangular prism
2. cone
3. cube
4. cylinder
5. 28
6. 279
7. 2,700
8. 1,800

Page 107
1. 2 lines
2. 3 lines
3. 1 line
4. 4 lines
5. yes
6. no
7. yes
8. no
9–12. Check drawings.
13. Answers will vary.
14. 13 pages
15. Check drawings.

Page 108
1–2. Check drawings.
3. slide
4. flip
5. turn
6. slide

7. two turns
8. 113 tiles
9. turn
10. slide
11. flip
12. turn

Page 109
1. rectangular prism
2. cylinder
3. pyramid
4. cone
5. sphere
6. triangular prism
7. pyramid
8. cone
9. rectangular prism
10. sphere, cylinder
11. rectangular prism
12. pyramid
13. cylinder
14. cone, cylinder
15. cylinder
16. June
17. Check drawings. Possible answer: a cube and a triangular prism

Page 110
1. 2 cm x 3 cm x 4 cm = 24 cubic cm
2. 5 cm x 3 cm x 5 cm = 75 cubic cm
3. 4 cm x 5 cm x 8 cm = 160 cubic cm
4. 6 cm x 7 cm x 1 cm = 42 cubic cm
5. 4 cm x 9 cm x 3 cm = 108 cubic cm
6. 5 cm x 2 cm x 6 cm = 60 cubic cm
7. 64 cubic cm
8. 30 cubic cm
9. 24 cubic cm
10. 3 cm
11. 6 cm
12. 8
13. 64
14. 27
15. 125

Page 111
1. Check drawings.
2. two-dimensional
3. three-dimensional
4. units
5. cubic units
6. square units

Page 112
1. part of a whole
2. part of a group
3. part of a whole
4. Ring first and third figures.
5. one half; one out of two; one divided by two
6. one eighth; one out of eight; one divided by eight
7. three fourths; three out of four; three divided by four
8. 8
9. $\frac{3}{8}$
10. $\frac{5}{8}$
11. 5 times

Page 113
1. $\frac{2}{5}$
2. $\frac{3}{4}$
3. $\frac{1}{2}$
4. $\frac{5}{8}$
5. $\frac{5}{6}$
6. $\frac{1}{6}$
7. 6
8. $\frac{5}{8}$ of the pie
9. 128 slices
10. $\frac{3}{5}$; $\frac{5}{5}$
11. $\frac{1}{3}$; $\frac{3}{3}$

Page 114
1. $\frac{1}{8}$
2. $\frac{1}{5}$
3. $\frac{3}{10}$
4. $\frac{1}{2}$
5. $\frac{0}{5}$
6. $\frac{9}{9}$
7. $\frac{3}{4}$
8. $2.64
9. $\frac{1}{10}$
10. $\frac{1}{20}$
11. $\frac{99}{100}$

Page 115
1. 8
2. 10
3. $\frac{3}{4}$
4. 2
5. 10
6. 3
7. 10
8. 12

Core Skills: Math, Grade 4, Answer Key (cont.)

Page 115 (cont.)
9. 3
10. 9 cards
11. 9 sports cars
12. 60 stamps
13. 96 rocks
14. $3
15. $12
16. $8

Page 116
1. $2.85
2. 36 baked goods
3. 11:15 A.M.
4. 3 times
Mixed Review
1. 1 line
   a. 0 lines
   b. 1 line
   c. 3 lines Ring b.
2. 16,520
3. 17,608
4. 28,294
5. 5,713
6. 16,694

Page 117
1. $\frac{2}{6}$
2. $\frac{2}{4}$
3. $\frac{6}{8}$
4. $\frac{1}{3}$
5. Ring last figure.
6. Ring third figure.
7–10. Answers will vary.
7. $\frac{2}{8}, \frac{3}{12}$
8. $\frac{2}{10}, \frac{3}{15}$
9. $\frac{4}{6}, \frac{6}{9}$
10. $\frac{6}{16}, \frac{9}{24}$
11. They eat the same amount.
12. 3 eggs
13–14. Answers will vary.
13. $\frac{24}{36}, \frac{12}{18}, \frac{4}{6}, \frac{2}{3}$
14. $\frac{8}{24}, \frac{4}{12}, \frac{2}{6}, \frac{1}{3}$

Page 118
1. $\frac{1}{3}$
2. $\frac{1}{4}$
3. $\frac{4}{5}$
4. $\frac{1}{6}$
5. $\frac{5}{6}$
6. $\frac{1}{4}$
7. $\frac{5}{6}, \frac{1}{2}$
8. $\frac{4}{4}, \frac{1}{5}$
9. $\frac{1}{7}$

10. $\frac{1}{6}$
11. $\frac{2}{7}$
12. $\frac{1}{3}$
13. $\frac{1}{2}$
14. $\frac{2}{3}$ hour
15. 8 hours
Mixed Review
1. 1,026
2. 4,470
3. 55 r2
4. 5,717
5. $0.05

Page 119
1. red
2. There are 6 white begonias.
3. 5 hours in the morning and 2 hours in the afternoon
4. September
5. 80 more pots
6. Problems will vary.

Page 120
1. $\frac{2}{6} < \frac{4}{6}$
2. $\frac{4}{5} > \frac{6}{10}$
3. $\frac{2}{4} = \frac{8}{16}$
4. <, like
5. >, unlike
6. <, like
7. >, like
8. <, unlike
9. >, unlike
10. $\frac{4}{10}, \frac{6}{10}, \frac{9}{10}$
11. $\frac{1}{6}, \frac{1}{2}, \frac{2}{3}, \frac{5}{6}$
12. Ming Lei
13. $\frac{1}{4}$ of the cookbooks
14. =
15. <
16. >
17. <

Page 121
1. $2\frac{5}{9}$
2. $1\frac{3}{8}$
3. $5\frac{1}{2}$
4. $5\frac{1}{2}$
5. $2\frac{1}{7}$
6. $1\frac{5}{9}$
7. $3\frac{1}{4}$
8. $3\frac{1}{3}$
9. $3\frac{1}{3}$ cups
10. $3\frac{1}{2}$ cans
11. $0.79

12. $3\frac{3}{4}$ cups
13. 2, $2\frac{1}{2}$, 3, $3\frac{1}{2}$
14. $1\frac{2}{3}$, 2, $2\frac{1}{3}$, $2\frac{2}{3}$
15. $1\frac{6}{7}$, $2\frac{2}{7}$, $2\frac{5}{7}$, $3\frac{1}{7}$

Page 122
1. about $\frac{1}{2}$
2. about 0
3. about 1
4–7. Drawings will vary.
4. about 2
5. about $1\frac{1}{2}$
6. about 1
7. about $\frac{1}{2}$
8. close to halfway
9. Becky
10. Answers will vary. Possible answers: 4, 8, 11, 13

Page 123
1. $\frac{6}{8}$, or $\frac{3}{4}$
2. $\frac{2}{3}$
3. $\frac{5}{8}$
4. $\frac{9}{10}$
5. $\frac{5}{6}$
6. $\frac{2}{3}$
7. $\frac{3}{4}$
8. $\frac{7}{8}$
9. $\frac{4}{5}$
10. $\frac{8}{10}$, or $\frac{4}{5}$
11. $\frac{5}{8}$
12. $\frac{7}{12}$
13. $\frac{1}{5}$
14. $\frac{1}{3}$
15. $\frac{6}{10}$

Page 124
1. $\frac{6}{9}$, or $\frac{2}{3}$
2. $\frac{1}{4}$
3. $\frac{5}{6}$
4. $\frac{1}{4}$
5. $\frac{1}{3}$
6. $\frac{1}{10}$
7. $\frac{2}{5}$
8. $\frac{5}{8}$
9. $\frac{1}{6}$
10. $\frac{7}{10}$
11. $\frac{3}{8}$
12. $\frac{5}{7}$
13. $\frac{6}{11}$

Core Skills: Math, Grade 4, Answer Key (cont.)

Page 124 (cont.)
14. $\frac{3}{9}$, or $\frac{1}{3}$
15. $\frac{2}{5}$
16. $\frac{6}{12}$, or $\frac{1}{2}$
17. $\frac{4}{7}$
18. $\frac{1}{6}$ box
19. close to no orange juice
20. $\frac{5}{12}$

Page 125
1. blue and yellow
2. $\frac{3}{4}$ of the quilt
3. $60.50
4. 40 books
Mixed Review
1. 9
2. 43
3. 14
4. 212
5. 379
6. 2
7. 3
8. 9
9. 2

Page 126
1. tenths
2. sixths
3. fourths
4. twelfths
5. ninths
6. eighths
7. $\frac{5}{6}$ of the lawn
8. $\frac{3}{3}$ hour; 60 minutes
9–11. Sample answers are given.
9. 6:00
10. 4:00
11. 9:00

Page 127
1. $\frac{7}{10}, \frac{5}{10}, \frac{2}{10}; \frac{1}{5}$
2. $\frac{1}{9}, \frac{3}{9}, \frac{4}{9}$
3. $\frac{5}{8}, \frac{2}{8}, \frac{7}{8}$
4. $\frac{10}{16}, \frac{10}{16}, \frac{0}{16}; 0$
5. $\frac{1}{4}$ cup
6. $\frac{5}{8}$ cup
7. 2, 4, 5, 8, 14, 23

Page 128
1. $3\frac{2}{8}$, or $3\frac{1}{4}$
2. $4\frac{7}{10}$

3. $6\frac{1}{6}$
4. $6\frac{2}{4}$, or $6\frac{1}{2}$
5. $4\frac{3}{4}$
6. $4\frac{4}{5}$
7. $2\frac{2}{6}$, or $2\frac{1}{3}$
8. $1\frac{7}{8}$ mi
9. $\frac{1}{8}$ mi longer
10. 8 times

Page 129
1. 3 in.; $2\frac{3}{4}$ in. or 3 in.; $2\frac{7}{8}$ in.
2. $2\frac{1}{2}$ in.; $2\frac{1}{4}$ in. or $2\frac{2}{4}$ in.; $2\frac{3}{8}$ in.
3–4. Answers will vary.
5. 50 feet
6. $\frac{3}{4}$ hour
7–9. Answers will vary.

Page 130
1. 2,648; 2,846; 6,248; 6,842; 8,246; 8,642
2. 9 choices
3. less than $10.00
4. 30 British stamps
5. Jorge, Diego, John, Dan, Bob, Geraldo
6. 12 dinner choices
7. Answers will vary.

Page 131
1. $\frac{1}{6}$
2. $\frac{1}{3}$
3. $\frac{1}{6}$
4. $\frac{1}{3}$
5. $\frac{1}{3}$
6. $\frac{4}{9}$
7. $\frac{2}{9}$
8. a red marble
9. a quarter; a nickel
10. $\frac{2}{6}$, or $\frac{1}{3}$
11. $\frac{3}{5}$
12. 5 cards

Page 132
1–2. Check diagrams.
1. 8 possibilities
2. 6 possibilities
3. 3 quarts
4. They picked the same amount.

Mixed Review
1. $\frac{1}{6}$
2. $\frac{1}{6}$
3. $\frac{1}{4}$
4. $\frac{5}{12}$
5. $\frac{1}{2}$
6. $\frac{5}{6}$
7. $3\frac{2}{8}$, or $3\frac{1}{4}$
8. $\frac{2}{9}$
9. $7\frac{4}{7}$
10. $2\frac{4}{6}$, or $2\frac{2}{3}$
11. $2\frac{6}{8}$, or $2\frac{3}{4}$

Page 133
1–6. Check drawings.
1. sixteen hundredths
2. five tenths
3. seventy-five hundredths
4. eight tenths
5. one and forty-two hundredths
6. one and seven hundredths
7. 0.4
8. 0.22
9. 4.86
10. 2.6
11. 0.05
12. 0.7
13. 1.5, 1.6, 1.7, 1.8
14. 2.16, 2.19, 2.25, 2.28
15. 46.45, 46.50, 46.55, 46.70

Page 134
1. $\frac{7}{10}$; 0.7
2. $\frac{78}{100}$; 0.78
3. $2\frac{5}{10}$; 2.5
4. $1\frac{86}{100}$; 1.86
5. 12.3
6. 18.70
7. 0.02
8. 6.9
9. 16.2
10. 8.6
11. 10.99
12. $\frac{65}{100}$
13. 26.07
14. $3\frac{1}{10}$
15. 3.3
16. $3\frac{5}{10}$
17. 3.7
18. $3\frac{9}{10}$

Core Skills: Math, Grade 4, Answer Key (cont.)

Page 135
1. 72 stamps
2. $7.00
3. 486
4. $18.70
5. $48
6. Yuki

Mixed Review
1. $\frac{4}{5}$
2. $\frac{2}{6}$, or $\frac{1}{3}$
3. $\frac{4}{8}$, or $\frac{1}{2}$
4. $\frac{4}{9}$
5. $\frac{6}{10}$, or $\frac{3}{5}$
6. $\frac{4}{12}$, or $\frac{1}{3}$

Page 136
1. 0.8; 0.80
2. 0.4; 0.40
3. 0.3; 0.30
4. 0.6; 0.60
5. 1.9; 1.90
6. 2.2; 2.20
7. 0.7
8. 6.80
9. 3.20
10. 0.1
11. 48.50 acres
12. 12 cows
13. 0.80, or 0.8
14. 0.27
15. 0.35
16. 0.50, or 0.5

Page 137
1. <
2. >
3. >
4. <
5. >
6. <
7. =
8. <
9. 5.8; 5.62; 3.5; 0.46
10. 52.43; 52.41; 51.75; 51.7
11. Beatrice; Carmen
12. Joseph
13. 76.54
14. 45.67

Page 138
1. 3.7; 3.8; 4.1; 4.2; 4.4
2. 8
3. 10
4. 2
5. 1
6. 21
7. 14

8. 24
9. 53
10. 5.9 km
11. 13 km
12. rounded
13. exact
14. rounded
15. exact

Page 139
1. 7
2. 2
3. 19
4. 4
5. 24
6. 13
7. 8
8. 40
9. 52
10. 30
11. 18 km
12. 3 minutes
13. $24.00; yes
14. $16.00; about $2.00

Page 140
1. 2.8; 0.44
2. 1.04; 0.56
3–7. Check place-value charts.
3. 23.51
4. 55.61
5. 5.4
6. 2.4
7. 5.82

Mixed Review
1. 8
2. 7, 1
3. 64
4. 1, 3
5. $1\frac{5}{8}$ in.
6. $2\frac{1}{8}$ in.

Page 141
1–2. Estimates may vary. One possible estimate is given.
1. about $92
2. about 35 km
3. 6 choices
4. 3 red vases and 7 white vases, or 7 red vases and 4 white vases
5. Answers will vary.

Page 142
1. 0.82
2. 24.3
3. 5.52
4. 9.32

5. 52.5
6. 6.81
7. 58.51
8. 42.38
9. 26.90
10. 26.12
11. 11.29
12. 8.05
13. 24.4
14. 56.54
15. 100.05 kg
16. 2 packages for $9.04
17. Cross out 7.05 and 7.55.
18. Cross out 90.4, 9.04, and 9.2.
19. Cross out 6.3, 6.6, and 60.6.

Page 143
1. 5.3
2. 3.31
3. 2.38
4. 3.64
5. 5.39
6. 16.07
7. 38.11
8. 37.77
9. 1.91
10. 8.51
11. 3.86
12. 6.5
13. 5.84
14. 22.09
15. 22.95 seconds
16. 63.82 seconds
17. 1.4 seconds
18. 69.87 seconds
19. Answers will vary.

Page 144
1. $12 \div 3 = 4$
2. $16 \div 2 = 8$
3. $28 \div 4 = 7$
4. $30 \div 5 = 6$
5–6. Check models.
5. $n = 5$
6. $n = 2$
7–10. Check place-value charts.
7. 6, 6, 60
8. 9, 9, 90
9. 5, 5, 50
10. 8, 8, 8
11. =
12. <
13. =
14. >

Core Skills: Math, Grade 4, Answer Key (cont.)

Page 145
1. 180
2. 60
3. 40, 5
4. 70, 3
5. 320, 8
6. 400, 8
7–16. Estimates will vary. Possible answers are given.
7. 2
8. 9
9. 7
10. 3
11. 8
12. 5
13. 2
14. 7
15. 6
16. 8
17. about 40 video games
18. 8 shelves
19. Answers may vary. Possible answer: The cartons that hold 22 tapes would be best, since the tapes would exactly fill 8 boxes. There would be no tapes remaining and no extra box needed.

Page 146
1. 3 hours
2. $105
3. 1 hour 1 minute
4. $166
5. one 12-pack; four 16-packs
6. $1.99
Mixed Review
1–9. Estimates may vary.
1. 600
2. 200
3. 1,200
4. 3,600
5. 800
6. 900
7. 600
8. 700
9. 800

Page 147
1–5. Check work.
6–9. Estimates will vary. Possible answers are given.
6. 2 r8
7. 4 r8
8. 5 r31
9. 5 r18
10. 7 r15

11. 6 r20
12. 9 cartons
13. $70
14. $0.06; $0.02; $0.05; $0.10; $0.20; $0.25; $0.29

Page 148
1. 4 r1
2. 4 r2
3. 3 r1
4. 3 r7
5. 5 r3
6. 4 r1
7. 2 r57
8. 5
9. 5 r17
10. 4 r8
11. 7 r10
12. 5 r20
13. 7
14. 6 r9
15. 9 r20
16. 6 r2
17. Answers will vary.

Page 149
1. 2
2. 5 r23
3. 5
4. 7
5. 4 r2
6. 5
7. 7
8. 7
9. 6
10. 8 r6
11. 6 r1
12. 4
13. 8
14. 6
15. 7 r9
16. 4 r4
17. 5,936 people
18. 3 subway cars
19. Answers will vary.
   Possible answers:
   $n = 250$, $x = 5$;
   $n = 1,250$, $x = 25$;
   $n = 400$, $x = 8$;
   $n = 1,000$, $x = 20$;
   $n = 1,500$, $x = 30$;
   $n = 600$, $x = 12$

Page 150
1. 9 rows
2. 10 photographs
3. 8 bags
4. 16 weeks

5. no
6. $0.65
7. 8 bunches
8. 6 tickets

Page 151
1–5. Check work.
6. 2; 2 r11
7. 4; 3 r49
8. 4; 4 r7
9. 2; 2 r9
10. 28 r9
11. 16 r6
12. 12 r16
13. 15 r22
14. 1,300 rolls; 3,276 rolls; 19 rolls; 5,564 rolls
15. Answers will vary.

Page 152
1. 36
2. 6
3. 23
4. 12
5. 28
6. 29
7. 14
8. 9
9. 28
10. 23
11. 23 snapshots
12. $2,760
13. 13, 9, 18
14. 200 hours
15. $2.00; $3.00; $11.00; $7.00